The Anatomy of
Mental Illness

The Anatomy of Mental Illness

Arthur Janov, Ph.D.

A BERKLEY MEDALLION BOOK
PUBLISHED BY
BERKLEY PUBLISHING CORPORATION

*This book is dedicated to the alleviation
of the suffering of mankind.*

CONTENTS

ACKNOWLEDGMENTS

I am indebted to Lee Woldenberg, M.D., for his help on the section "The Neurophysiology of Mental Illness." His editorial help as well as the formulation of important concepts was essential to the development of that discussion. Editorial suggestions by Professor Bernard Campbell of Cambridge helped make the neurophysiology section more readable. Finally, thanks to the person who literally put this book together on paper, my typist, Joanne Barnett.

Primal Therapy should not be practiced by anyone who is not qualified to do so. The only person qualified to practice Primal Therapy is someone with a certificate as a Primal Therapist from the Primal Institute in Los Angeles.

INTRODUCTION

Several years have passed since the discovery of Primal Therapy and an almost equal number of years since I began the book *The Primal Scream*. A great deal has happened in those intervening years to the theory, to the patients, and to the science of Primal Therapy. In this work I plan to detail those happenings.

When *The Primal Scream* first appeared, there was an understandable skepticism among professionals. That book was never intended as a scientific document; rather, it was an attempt to share with the public what I believed to be a remarkable discovery, something that would mean the end of suffering for many human beings. *The Anatomy of Mental Illness* is designed to provide new understandings that have developed since *The Primal Scream* by:

1. Providing the neurophysiologic background for Primal Theory.

2. Integrating Primal Theory into the mainstream of what is known in science about the brain and its functions.

3. Presenting advanced aspects of the theory.

4. Providing follow-up studies of patients who have had the therapy.

5. Clarifying the origins of symptoms and how they develop, so that further insights can be gained in the area of psychosomatic medicine.

6. Supplying research data on Primal patients to accurately measure the changes that come about as a result of the therapy.

One might wonder why a social scientist would present a scientific theory to the public first and scientists second, since nearly always the reverse is the custom. Aside from my ordinarily perverse nature, there are some sound reasons for this choice. Psychotherapy is not just a science (if we grant that any science of psychotherapy has ever existed); it is a profession, staffed by individuals who make a living from it. And it is unrealistic to expect someone who has spent a good part of his life learning a profession to suddenly give up what he is doing because someone has another idea of how to practice it. The history of organized professions is filled with attempts to suppress the new, the unconventional, and the unorthodox. I brought my findings to the people, and they responded. It is the great response of suffering humans all over the globe which has forced the recalcitrant professionals to take another look, to open their minds and see the possibilities in this new therapy.

But Primal Therapy and Primal Theory must stand the test of science; and it is to both scientists and knowledgeable laymen that I address this book. Primal Therapy has moved quite heavily into the area of research. There is now a fully equipped research laboratory at the Primal Institute in Los Angeles where research on patients proceeds day and night. Daily measurements are made of the brains and bodies of selected patients, dreams are monitored, and brain waves are investigated during sleep and immediately before and after each therapy session. Some of the findings are presented later on in this work. What we have found thus far confirms the initial optimism about the efficacy of the techniques. It is certainly exciting to me to see the way we are altering brain waves in a permanent way, for it indicates that reliving a Primal Scene really does make significant biologic changes. When body temperature drops after a Primal, we again find validation of this important notion—namely, that blocked Pain produces permanent tension, and feeling it eradicates that tension. Carefully controlled studies are under way that indicate it is not the physical activity, or suggestion, or the relationship to the therapist that makes for those biologic changes—it is the Primal experience.

Primal Theory and Primal Therapy are open systems. The Primal Therapy of today is far different from that of a year ago, and I know it will be far different a year from now. Old patients would scarcely recognize the therapy now, yet the basic suppositions and hypotheses have changed little. They have been elaborated and expanded into a more comprehensive and extensive theory, generating universal laws of human development.

We have had a chance to take a longer view of the patients in this therapy. Some of them have now been out of the therapy for years. What they have to say about themselves and the therapy is reported in a preliminary study in this book. Not one patient who has gone through Primal Therapy would ever again consider any other kind of treatment. That is important subjective evidence for the power and efficacy of the method. We have had our failures; and our plan is to study them as soon as possible. By and large, they are individuals who left therapy prematurely—who felt that the Pain was too much and decided that a life of neurosis was preferable. But the failure rate is very small indeed. Even in our so-called failures, there have been significant biologic changes in terms of heart rate, blood pressure, core body temperature, etc. But the fact remains that some patients do leave too early. For some, it is not easy to go on feeling Pain month after month, although not infrequently patients will return after a hiatus.

If I were to try to explain why this book came after *The Primal Scream*, I would say that I wanted to reach the hearts of people before their heads. That is, I wanted people to understand that feelings validate, and that if something felt right it was likely to be right. I wanted people to trust their feelings and themselves and not search for validation in the cerebral flummery of theoreticians. Of the thousands of people who seek entry into the Institute each month, only the professionals want to know facts first. And no matter how many facts we offer, there is always more they want to know, because they can never know enough to make them feel. Professionals have a right to know more—and that is the purpose of this book—but if they do not *feel*, facts won't change their outlook or their clinical approach.

Part of the problem has been that psychology has been a mental science, and psychologists have been mental specialists, when we should have understood that the mind is not something split off from the body to be dissected and analyzed as a separate entity. Psychology is the study of feelings—the particular relationship of mental events to brain and body processes, and the relationship of bodily changes and their effects on the mind—in short, the study of whole man. To feel is to understand the prepotency of feelings in the psychological schemata.

The reader will again find case histories to accompany the theory. I believe in the unity of theory and practice. If the theory is plausible and well integrated yet of no use to humanity, I would consider it has but minimal value. The truth of a theory of psychology lies not only in its statistical data but its ability to help human beings. If Primal Theory about sleep and dreams is correct, it should explain why some of us do not sleep well, why we have nightmares, and what it would take to enjoy restful sleep. Just that, a good night's sleep, would be a welcome event to many millions of people.

I am convinced that Primal Therapy can be likened to the "Fountain of Youth" we have been searching for—the way to prolong life. The greatly lowered body temperature, the much less active brain, the slower metabolic rate, the absence of neurotic tension and the diseases it brings, must add decades to our lives.*

The more we see of the dramatic changes in Primal Therapy, the more gratified we become. Those who perform the therapy believe it is the most exciting work imaginable. We sometimes feel overwhelmed by the crush of applications and demands of a suffering humanity. We know that we could never begin to help more than a scintilla of those in need, even though we give preference to professionals in order to expand our staff What is required is an *organized* societal approach: backing by governmental agencies and, finally, support by the professionals. This support is now gaining momentum: in one city, an entire community, along with its mayor, is gearing itself to a total Primal approach to the problems of drug addiction, crime, and other neuroses.

It is assumed that the reader of this book has a familiarity with Primal concepts, as presented in *The Primal*

*Professor Bernard Strehler helped confirm this point at the summer, 1971, Biologic meeting in Switzerland when he told the conference that a drop of 3.6 degrees in body temperature would "almost certainly extend the human life span by twenty years."

Scream. However, for those who need to refresh themselves on the basic tenets of Primal Theory, I have included a general outline of the theory as a prologue. What you will read here in *The Anatomy of Mental Illness* is just a beginning. But I feel it is a good start.

THE ANATOMY OF MENTAL ILLNESS:
The Scientific Basis of Primal Therapy

Primal Theory

Antonin Artaud was a French actor and theater organizer. He was born in 1896, and he lived for fifty-two years. Nine of these years he spent in insane asylums. He believed that the function of the theater is revolutionary; a play should help remake the world, not entertain. "The spectator should not leave the theatre yawning or smiling but shocked and terrified, like someone who has seen his wife undergo an open-heart operation or witnessed genocide in Biafra. You must go to the theatre as you would to a surgeon, insisted Artaud—gravely, knowing that you will not leave intact." [1]

His idea of a theater was one with uncomfortable seats that would collapse if the spectators fell asleep. Foul smells, he promised, would waft through the aisles during the performance.

"In 1933 there took place one of the most bizarre lectures ever given at the Sorbonne; it was Artaud discussing 'The Theatre and the Plague.' He was seated at a desk, with a blackboard framing his lean face. The corners of his mouth were stained black from laudanum, and when he spoke, his long-fingered hands flapped like a bird's wings, and hair fell over his massive brow. Like the plague, Artaud began, the theatre must contain the thrust of an epidemic. The plague creates a second state in which social order is abolished and the members of the community respond to deep unconscious urges; the miser throws gold out of windows, and the solemn bourgeois is seized by an erotic fever. The theatre, too, must be a crisis resolved by death or cure, it must push men to see themselves as they are. It must make the masks fall, uncover lies, baseness, and hypocrisy, and reveal to the community its dark powers and its hidden strengths." [2]

In front of an audience of intellectuals at the Sorbonne, Artaud lost control of what he was saying and became

[1] Sanche de Gramont, "A Vocation for Madness," *Horizons*, Vol. XII, No. 2 (Spring, 1970), pp. 49–55.
[2] *Ibid.*

a victim of the plague. "He let go of the thread we were following and began to act out dying by plague. . . . His face was contorted with anguish, and one could see the perspiration dampening his hair. His eyes dilated, his muscles became cramped, his fingers struggled to retain their flexibility. He made you feel the parched and burning throat, the pains, the fever, the fire in the gut." [3]

The audience laughed at the impromptu performance, and many left. Artaud told Anaïs Nin: "They want to hear an obective lecture on 'The Theatre and the Plague,' and I want to give them the experience itself, . . . so they will be terrified, and awaken." [4]

All of us are born with certain basic needs—to be fed when hungry, to be kept warm, to have privacy, to be stimulated and held, and to be allowed to develop in accordance with our natural abilities. These indigenous needs I call Primal needs. They are essential human requirements. Not to fulfill any of these needs, not to hold a child sufficiently or to feed him on a schedule instead of when he is hungry, means to deny Primal needs and produce pain. The pain resulting from the denial of Primal need I term Primal Pain. Primal Pains result from the many ways a child is not allowed to be himself. They result when a child is forced to walk too soon or when he is encouraged to talk before he is ready. Later, when verbal skills develop, it can mean not allowing him to speak his thoughts and feelings. These suppressed feelings become needs as potent as any biological ones until they are felt, expressed, and resolved.

Any early need which goes unfulfilled produces a lingering tension in the body which propels it toward fulfillment and, finally, rest or relaxation. If the need or the need-feeling cannot be fulfilled or resolved—if the child is not allowed to cry, for example—then tension remains. One does not get over unfulfilled needs just as one does not get over the pains of their denial. These pains remain encapsulated in the human system, producing layers of

[3] *The Diary of Anaïs Nin, 1931–1934* (New York: Harcourt, Brace & World, 1966), p. 191.
[4] *Ibid.*, p. 192.

tension (which is how the pain is experienced) which build progressively, requiring one outlet or another. But discharge of tension is *not* eradication—no matter how many drinks one has or how many times he masturbates, Primal Pain will not disappear.

Early Primal needs are not continuously experienced if they go unheeded. Rather, a point is reached in the fragile young organism where the pain of chronic unfulfillment shuts down even the experience of the need or the feeling. If to express a feeling brings punishment or indifference, then sooner or later that expression will be suppressed. Years of such suppression can produce a state in which the feelings are no longer recognizable. Even when they are recognized, they become so deeply buried that they cannot be felt by any act of will.

We see, then, that the young organism shuts off excessive pain automatically by shunting out of conscious awareness and away from direct physical experience anything that has become intolerable and threatens the ongoingness of the system. As pain mounts, as he is forbidden to explore, to say, to do, the child must split away or disconnect himself from his needs. This means that he is becoming a split person—split between his real self and the front he must maintain for his parents; as, for example, being polite and respectful. Unless some catastrophic event takes place early in the child's life, the splitting process develops slowly, making him increasingly shut off and unreal. There comes a day when an event takes place, not necessarily traumatic in and of itself, in which a shift is made from simply a child with certain suppressions to one who has effectively turned a good part of himself off. That is, the leap is made from a suppressed child to a neurotic child. In this state the balance has shifted so that the unreal self predominates and the child cannot recall and experience his real self.

The event which produces this leap into neurosis is usually only an end point, a culmination—the last straw. It can happen when the child is left with a baby-sitter for the hundredth time or when his mother says once again, "If you ever say that again I'll send you away." This critical event I call the major Primal Scene. It is an event in which the child begins to make sense out of the first five or six years of his existence, the time when he can begin to generalize and classify all his previous experiences. It is when for one fleeting moment he sees that he cannot be himself and expect to be loved by his parents. Undefended children do see the truth readily, but when a realization occurs that is catastrophic for them, that realization together with a clear perception of reality must be instantly denied. It is not usually any conscious process; rather, the organism reacts automatically to preserve its integrity. The child slips into neurosis without a flicker of recognition of what has happened to him. He becomes what he must in order to survive with his parents. He will stop crying, stop sassing, stop saying what is on his mind, without a conscious effort. That is the difference between neurosis and being somewhat suppressed. A young child who is just suppressed usually knows what he feels—say, angry—and he holds it back with an effort. He no longer throws that tantrum because of the beating which would ensue. But when he becomes neurotic, there is no conscious effort required to hold himself back. A barrier has been constructed against his real self which does the job effortlessly.

Primal needs become painful when unattended. Thus when the organism shuts away the pain it also shuts off the need. The feelings and needs then become stored in the memory system, sending impulses to the body, keeping it chronically tense. Those pains remain for a lifetime as pristine, vivid, and hurtful as the day they began. Tension is the pressure of such pains disconnected from awareness. When they become connected, the pain and the feeling is identified for what it is and tension disappears. The pain and its experience as tension cannot be undone by any single behavior, by meditation, yoga, pills, cigarettes, alcohol, or even psychotherapy. The pains can be undone only when they are made into full human experiences; that is, when they are relived one by one until they are resolved and out of the system. Perhaps a more accurate way of stating this is that the experiences must be lived, not *relived*, since they were never entirely experienced in the first place; which is why they persisted.

Living out these pains is to experience the self more and more fully until one simply becomes what he is—a completely experiencing human being, living the "now" of life instead of trying to resolve the past in a myriad of ways.

So long as need is not felt with its pain, the organism must be driven to act in unreal or symbolic ways. It is very much like having your motor turned on early in life and not being able to turn it off again no matter what you do. For example, not being held and caressed as an infant produces a need to be held. This may be acted out symbolically through compulsive sex. This behavior may well occur without any specific memory of not being held early in life. The infant simply hurts and has a desperate need. This need may be acted out randomly in the first few months and years of life; thus he may wet the bed, soil himself, suck his thumb, cry incessantly, or throw up continuously. To treat the result, the symptoms of the need, is to miss the point and solve nothing except to force the infant to find new outlets. If the child should try to find substitute satisfaction through overeating (because real satisfactions were nonexistent), this behavior is symbolic. That is, it is fulfilling a real, though unconscious, need symbolically. It is unceasing neurotic conduct because it is only a symbolic satisfaction, and to treat overeating is to miss the impelling force underlying it.

It will do no good for the neurotic to "figure out" his needs or to analyze his feelings and handle them. Needs do not disappear because they are understood. They disappear when they are felt; and they can be felt only when the person can safely experience them; that is, when he is no longer dependent on his parents for life. What I am saying is that needs are not a pocket in the brain which one becomes aware of—making the unconscious conscious—and dispels. Needs are total tissue states. When we are not held early in life, that deprivation isn't just a memory; it is a deprivation of our entire being. That is how it must be experienced—totally.

The only truth is experienced truth; and human truth is idiosyncratic. There is a single set of hurts which is specific to each of us. No one has to interpret what those hurts are for us, because interpretation is simply someone else's version of reality and can be falsified or misjudged. To feel the hurt is to know all there is to know about why one acted in this way or that.

The job of therapy, then, is not to interpret but to aid someone to experience—to connect his history with his behavior.

What, then, is neurosis? Neurosis is the symbolization of Primal Pain. To defend against pain is, by definition, to act symbolically, because to feel the pain is to be real —to feel one's needs and to attempt to satisfy them in real ways.

I believe that shutting down against pain is a reflexive act, and that neurosis is a genetic legacy which aids in the survival of the human species. Without neurosis for protection, the child faced with catastrophic reality ("I will never be loved as long as I live") might well go crazy or be unable to continue as a viable being.

When neurosis outlives its usefulness it doesn't just fade away, unfortunately. It keeps us unconscious of pain even when we could withstand the knowledge that our parents despised us. Neurosis is not discriminating; it is like a guest who remains forever, long outliving his welcome. The only way we can get it to leave is to feel what is below its protective shield. It developed slowly, remember, by dint of day-by-day insults, assaults, humiliations, degradations, suppressions, indifferences—hurt after hurt. It is undone in reverse order; feeling those hurts in sequence beginning with the most tolerable and traveling to the most intolerable.

Fortunately, we do not have to relive each and every hurt. There are key scenes which represent the feelings involved in many similar events. These scenes are known as Primal Scenes. There will be a memory, for instance, of one of father's tirades and the feeling of terror of his temper. Reliving that scene will evoke automatically other similar terrors of the father. The reliving of that Primal Scene will produce violent thrashing, even convulsive behavior, just because it unleashes *all* of the early terror. Experiencing that tower of terror is earthshaking and, in my opinion, curative, because it was the suppression of the fear which produced neurotic behavior—fear of all men, reticent, stammering, tentative conduct, the development of irrational ideas, etc. (Similarly, blocking the crying response over a period of years may produce a chronically running nose or blockage of the sinuses. When one cries the Primal cry, which may go on for hours and which is a cry felt from one's head to one's toes, the symbolic blockage of sinuses may clear away permanently.) During a Primal, which is the reliving of Primal Pains, a person may remember one event after another in which he needed to cry but could not, all the while being convulsed by tears. To have unleashed the crying response is to liberate all of the relevant old memories and scenes. This is why one may cry deeply for hours. Those hours of crying, however, may span two decades of suppressions and liberate those suppressions forever.

To block a Primal feeling is to try to solve that feeling in the present and to imagine that the feeling derives from something in the present. A young girl's terror of her father may drive her later to marry a man who is also quick-tempered. She may think she is afraid of her husband and struggle constantly to mollify him; what she is doing, however, is trying to convert her father, symbolically through her husband, into a less fear-producing person. She is trying to master old feelings by manipulating the present. She must do it symbolically with her husband, since she could not make her father a decent, gentle person. That father left her with her terror, which must be resolved in some way. This is why she doesn't marry a kind person in the first place, or why she doesn't leave her brutal husband. She needs the struggle so she can produce a better outcome symbolically.

Struggle is an important concept in Primal Theory because it is my contention that the neurotic becomes involved with people who can perpetuate his struggle—that is, with whom he can recreate his early life circumstances and struggle to produce symbolically a new outcome. Thus, he may marry a cold person and try to tease warmth out of her. Or she may marry a critical person and try to make him approving. These are obvious examples, but needless to say, the symbolic struggle can become quite complex and devious. An example is sexual perversion, in which a person must put himself through some elaborate painful ritual (perhaps of being tied to a chair and beaten with chains) in order to experience the feelings of his body.

What is important to remember is that no altering or satisfaction of symbolic behavior alters the neurotic pattern. A person who had a need to be listened to patiently by parents too flighty and/or preoccupied to do so may later lecture to thousands who sit listening attentively; and yet this need to be listened to will not change one iota. It will change only when the *reality* of feeling how he needed his parents' attention is experienced together with the pain of how little attention he received from them.

Why does a past need or feeling generalize to the present? Because it was not fully felt *specifically*. If a young child could have felt: "I'll never be loved by my *mother*," then he would not have covered over the hurt and tried unconsciously to get mother-love out of teachers, for example. The child would have felt a specific deprivation, something between him and his mother. Because the child cannot face and feel that he is unloved or disliked, he does what he can to fulfill the need vicariously. The need drives him to get love where he can; thus, his behavior generalizes to others. Or if his anger was blocked, that will be taken out on others in one way or another.

These other outlets are neurotic because they are symbolic of the original situation. The teacher is not a mother. The boss need not be feared as though he were the tyrannical father. To try to block the neurosis, such as compulsive talking, is only to build tension. Need is the matrix which incorporates each event; so a woman will say, "You have a nice dress on," and then follow it immediately with, "I've got to get one like it," or, "Take it from me. I'm the expert on clothes"—constant reference to a needing self.

Clearly, I view neurosis as the pathology of feeling. Conversely, to fully feel is to be well, in the Primal matrix. To feel means not to be plagued by chronic tension, not to be driven to find relief.

The neurotic does not learn and change from his experience, because he does not experience fully once he is split. That is, he does not experience the things that can free and change him—his Pains. Once he is split, we can address only his unreal front. We may rearrange that front (from delinquent to brain surgeon, from obese to skinny) without every changing the real internal sickness that lies below.

What the neurotic does not need, in my opinion, is any kind of confrontation either with a deity or with another loving or understanding human being. I do not think that we can love, punish, or placate neurosis out of existence. What the neurotic needs is to connect with himself—not to handle that self but to have unified and unifying experiences that mend the disconnection of thought from feeling, of mind from body. That is what is real—connection to oneself. Once connection is achieved and we merge with what is real inside us, then we can relate that humanness to others. In short, the process of cure always works from inside out and not vice versa.

I am calling for revolution. When you are going to overthrow a system, and neurosis is a sick system, you do not begin a dialogue with that system. Any dialogue, insight, or special perception will be incorporated into that sickness without changing it for a moment. We must overthrow that system by force and violence—the force of compressed needs and feelings which have remained hidden possibly for decades; the violence of wrenching them out of an unreal system.

For any revolution to endure, it must rest on a solid theory. Progressive revolutions *evolve* out of theory. There is no freedom in eschewing theory; only anarchy results from that; theory must be consciously directed. To be anchored solidly in theory is to be free to extrapolate and to make leaps into the realm of the possible. The more specifically Primal Theory is tied to neurophysiologic events, the more broad-ranged its ramifications. We shall now enter the rather forbidding area of neurophysiology to see if we can find out the nature of Pain, where it is processed, how it is blocked, and what happens when it is repressed. We shall discuss what repression really means in the brain and the body, which brain structures are involved in repression, and what it takes to "unrepress" someone. Essentially, the chapter on neurophysiology indicates that there are specific brain structures involved in the organization and storage of feeling, other brain systems active in repressing those feelings, and still other areas of the brain involved in symbolizing them. We will see that neurotic, symbolic thoughts are often a matter of literal distances from feeling sites in the brain—the more distant, the more symbolic. We will see how Pain drives feelings away from their proper mental connection toward symbolic hookups; and how feeling Pain produces a literal connection of one brain structure with another. Finally, we will note how making connections in the brain finally solves the historic plague of man—mental illness.

I. The Neurophysiology of Neurosis and Psychosis

"Microscopic forms of cardiac hemorrhages have become very frequent in recent years. They are not always fatal. Some people get over them. It's a typical modern disease. I think its causes are of a moral order. The great majority of us are required to live a life of constant, systematic duplicity. Your health is bound to be affected if, day after day, you say the opposite of what you feel, if you grovel before what you dislike and rejoice at what brings you nothing but misfortune. Our nervous system isn't just a fiction, it's a part of our physical body, and our soul exists in space and is inside us, like the teeth in our mouth. It can't be forever violated with impunity. I found it painful to listen to you, Innokentii, when you told us how you were re-educated and became mature in jail. It was like listening to a circus horse describing how it broke itself in."

BORIS PASTERNAK
Doctor Zhivago

Past psychologic theories have failed to become integrated with basic neurophysiology, and therefore have been divorced from the physical substrate of the mind and its pathology—neurosis. The fact that we are psychophysiologic beings requires a theory that encompasses a total thinking-feeling being. Only a holistic theory can move us beyond post-hoc rationalizations into a scientific, predictive psychology.

The importance of biologic functioning in psychologic theory is made clear when we make a statement such as, "He repressed his feelings." This implies a distinct section of the brain involved with feelings, another section dealing with repression, and posits an interaction between the two in a concrete physical way. Any psychologic statement, therefore, is ultimately a neurologic one. It is therefore important that we understand the brain in neurosis.

25

The dialectic principle is the interpretation of opposites. This means that in every specific case there is the general, and in the general is stated the specific. To understand one brain is to understand brains in general, and to understand the functioning of brains is to know how a single brain works. If neurosis is the dysfunction of brain, then to understand a single neurosis is to understand the *structure* of all neuroses. Simply to know about neurotic *responses* does not mean one knows about the basic structure of neurosis. Though the response forms are complex, I believe that neurosis itself is a single pathologic process, and if this is so, the treatment for "the" neurosis may be single and specific as well, no matter what form it takes.

The integration of the psychologic with its neurologic counterparts is what makes a psychologic theory solid, predictive, and finally, of therapeutic value. This integration is what I intend to bring about in the following presentation.

1. THE BASIS FOR NEUROSIS

Unmet Needs

Throughout man's evolution there have been constant external dangers. He has dealt with these threats in much the same way as his reptilian ancestors, by fight or flight. Man no longer has to flee from wild animals, but his environment is no less hostile. Man must flee from himself. He is born into a situation where his needs cannot be met, where his feelings cannot be expressed spontaneously, and where he is not allowed to mature at his own natural pace. He rarely can be totally himself. In order to get by in his immediate social milieu, his family, he must often be something unnatural. He must inhibit his deepest needs and feelings because they constitute a danger—the danger of the loss of love, caring, and protection by his all-powerful parents. He must be quiet and polite, respectful, or whatever else his parents need him to be in order to dispense their protection. Their needs become his implicit commands. The danger is that in expressing himself, he will possibly lose those whom he needs in order to survive. This danger grows more apparent early in life when the child feels for an epiphanic moment that to be real, to be himself, is never to have his needs met. He can never be loved for being himself— his open, spontaneous, free-feeling and acting self. He must put a barrier against himself, the feeling self, which is rejected. In so doing, the child finds himself in conflict.

The Conflict

The conflict, briefly (and simplified), originates as follows: The motivating need is often diencephalic—perhaps from the hunger center of the hypothalamus. If this need is unfulfilled (for any number of reasons), the pain of the unmet need is stored in the temporal cortex. The frontal cortex acts continuously to prevent this unconscious material from becoming conscious, and the battleground for this conflict is the limbic system.

Thus, the *feeling* of danger is processed in the limbic system, while the *realization*, the catastrophic comprehension of the danger, is formulated elsewhere—in the frontal cortex. In Primal Theory, this disengagement is called the "split," or the "disconnection." In other words, we can separate our consciousness from our feelings so that we eventually do not know what hurts us, or even that we hurt. We are no longer conscious of the danger— the feeling or action which spells danger—even though that danger is being processed below the level of awareness. In an experiment by Gaunt, rats were put under stress (tied to a board) and then given tranquilizers. Tranquilized rats seemed indifferent to their situation, but their bodies still produced a marked increase in the output of a stress hormone (ACTH).[1]

Similarly, in experiments with hypnotized persons, a pinprick and other painful stimuli were introduced to subjects under hypnosis. Though they reported no conscious experience of pain, electroencephalographic tracings indicated that their systems were under stress. Neither

[1] R. Gaunt et al., *Brain Mechanisms and Drug Action*, ed. by William S. Fields (Springfield, Ill.: Charles Thomas Co., 1957), p. 105.

drugs nor consciousness-suppressing techniques such as hypnosis can make the body lie. This indicates that stress may continue in the system without any consciousness of it.

According to Primal Theory, the human system can tolerate pain consciously only to certain levels. At certain critical levels the system automatically shuts off and renders us unconscious of that pain. A literal translation of this is fainting, in which extreme physical pain causes unconsciousness. The pain continues to affect us, however, pushing the system into an overload situation where the tension must be acted upon. One of the best releases is to scream and yell. If, however, screaming is opprobrious and brings with it more pain (more threats of rejection or lack of love), it will be suppressed.[2]

When a child is born into a neurotic family, his pain begins. Often it begins at birth with a long and hard (and often drugged) labor in a neurotic mother. It continues with lack of sufficient breast feeding, moves on to hurried toilet training, suppression of natural curiosity and noise making, and, finally, to suppression of words and feelings which do not conform to the parents' moral value system. Add to this the pain of surgery or other catastrophic afflictions. The body does not distinguish between its pains, and the physiologic process of pain is the same whether the origin is psychologic or physical (as in the case of surgery). We defend against any overwhelming pain, but the residue remains in the system unresolved. The residue builds, depending on the amount of pain undergone, psychologic and physiologic. At certain critical levels the child, because of overwhelming pain, becomes split off from his feeling self, because to feel is to open the gate to all pain and to be overwhelmed by it.

Neurosis and the Withdrawal from Pain

Neurosis is the result of the disconnection. It is the form by which the child, and later the adult, acts out (or in) the overload. One child may bang his head chronically, another suck his thumb, and yet another fight con-

[2] Arthur Janov, *The Primal Scream* (New York: G. P. Putnam's Sons, 1970). See this for overall Primal Theory.

tinuously with his peers. Neurosis, then, is the rechanneled energy of the feeling into outlets.

The disconnection is an active process. The feelings and their pain are continuously actively inhibited. This process is called repression and is automatic and unconscious. There are specific areas of the brain which mediate this repression and keep us unconscious of ourselves and our pain.

We see that neurosis is a literal brain dysfunction, a split in the neurologic unity. Lord Russell Brain points this out:

> The ever changing content of the brain in action, particularly of the cerebral cortex, must equally be variable. If there are nodal areas, they must surely be diencephalic, since it is in the brain-stem and diencephalon that the neural bases of attention, emotion and memory seem most closely related to one another . . . cortex and diencephalon need to be regarded not as a hierarchy, but as an integrative unity.[3]

The withdrawal from pain is common to all forms of organic life. The one-celled amoeba withdraws when irritated and can discriminate between something needed, such as food, and things harmful, such as noxious chemicals. Fish quickly learn to avoid water where the temperature is not suitable, and humans in a light coma will raise their hands reflexively to pull away from a painful stimulus. This latter point suggests that we can feel and react to pain even on an unconscious level and that withdrawal from pain is a survival reflex in humans as well. The disengagement of one area of brain from another (repression) is no more than an extension of the survival mechanism beginning with the sensitivity to pain or irritation shown by the one-celled amoeba. Indeed, neurotic brain dysfunction is but an aggregate of cells functioning in a complex way. What is true for a single cell also may be true of cells in aggregate. The amoeba withdraws from external irritations, while the brain is able to withdraw from internal ones. In this sense, the ability to repress

[3] Russell Brain, "Some Reflections on Brain and Mind," *Brain*, Vol. 86, Part 3 (Sept., 1963), p. 399.

and become neurotic is a genetic legacy which allows the human to go on coping with his external milieu despite the fact that his body is being ravaged internally.

Contraction against pain, and relaxation when it is absent, seems to be a fundamental process encompassing all organic matter. E. H. Hess investigated pupillary reactions and found that the pupil dilates when the stimulus is pleasant and contracts when it is unpleasant.[4] When the subjects in the Hess experiments were presented with pictures of torture scenes, there was an automatic and involuntary pupillary constriction. The brain, then, stores the memory of pain, and the body will react *as though in pain* when the memory is aroused. We see, also, that we withdraw not only from external pain but from internally prompted pain. Memory can bring about the withdrawal or constriction process against pain, as though the pain were external.

The pupillary constriction which took place in the experimental subjects could be brought about by the remembrance of feelings—feelings evidently too painful to accept and integrate normally. From this we can see that feelings can be responded to unconsciously in a physiologic way and can produce not only constriction of the pupils but also contraction of the blood vessels and, finally, the narrowing of consciousness away from the source of pain.

I believe that Primal Pains, overwhelming feelings from childhood which could not be integrated—"They don't like me as I am"—remain in the system, producing a continuous withdrawal of consciousness and a stabilized neurosis. When the brain (and the body) withdraws from painful feelings, we are left with undelineated nervous activity, experienced as amorphous tension which con-

---

[4] E. H. Hess and J. M. Polt, "Pupil Size in Relation to Interest Value of Visual Stimuli," *Science*, Vol. 132 (1960), pp. 347–350. It should be added that when man is in danger, his pupils dilate owing to the constriction of the ciliary muscles of the eye. Dilation here serves the survival purpose of opening the organism for the purpose of processing more information and thus protecting itself. In the Hess experiments there was an overload of stimulation that could not be smoothly integrated without constriction.

stantly mobilizes the system to act in one way or another. This tension is the disconnected (from consciousness) portion of the feeling—the energy source, as it were, which causes rechanneled behaviors, behaviors which I call neurotic because they are driven by repressed feelings.

The existence of such an energy source is established by neurophysiologists. W. H. Gantt, in describing responses of the organism in terms of basic physiologic reflexes, notes: "The emotional basis for action remains after the external and superficial movements of adaptation have been lost. . . . The organism [is then] pounded by past emotional memories which prepare it for an act no longer required."[5] Because we are pounded by early unresolved memories, which I call "Primal," we must continuously defend against them so that they do not become conscious and overpower us.

Primal Pains keep the human system activated. As Albe-Fessard points out, "Pain has the greatest arousal effect of any other form of peripheral stimulus."[6] This is necessary, since the arousal against pain is life-saving; it helps keep us alive, defended, and neurotic. The function of "unpleasure" is protective. To quote Gellhorn:

> All the recognized emotions may be considered from the standpoint of self-preservation and the preservation of the species. Emotions that are informative in regard to threats to self-preservation . . . are characteristically unpleasant in nature. On the other side are pleasurable emotions that are informative of the removal of threats, the active gratification of needs, and the temporary achievement of a state of internal and/or external homeostasis.[7]

Summary

Repression is the natural tranquilizer of the system. It is protective early in life when we are helpless and totally

---

[5] As reported in E. Gellhorn, *Biological Foundations of Emotion* (Chicago, Ill.: Scott, Foresman Co., 1968), p. 86.

[6] D. Bowsher and K. Albe-Fessard, "Patterns of Somatosensory Organization Within the Central Nervous System," in C. A. Keele, *Assessment of Pain in Man and Animals* (Edinburgh: Livingstone, 1961), p. 11.

[7] Gellhorn, *op. cit.*, p. 75.

dependent, and becomes pathologic when we are no longer in such a position. Full expression of feelings involves the total brain, both higher and lower centers. When the expression of feeling (which ordinarily would be protective, according to Gellhorn) *itself* becomes the threat—such as talking back in anger to one's parents—then those feelings must be isolated from consciousness, the conflict arises, and we become "split." In other words, a child responds angrily when he is hurt or has his needs frustrated. To make that angry response opprobrious is to impose a double burden on him; he cannot make the appropriate survival response because the response itself becomes life-threatening—the loss of parental love.

Thus we see that the withdrawal from pain is common to all forms of organic life from single-celled organisms to man. Man has evolved the most extensive and complicated system of all, and his large cerebral cortex maintains this complex neuronal reflex against injury—neurosis. We can now examine this process in more structural detail.

2. THE STRUCTURE OF NEUROSIS

The Reticular Activating System

The reticular activating system is part of the reticular formation, a diverse structure that extends from the lower brainstem into the midbrain to end at the thalamus and cortex. It is supplied throughout its length by collaterals from nerves on their way to the sensory cortex. It is safe to say that all sensory inputs from the external environment, such as smell, taste, touch, sight, and hearing, relay information here on the way to finer discrimination in various parts of the neocortex. But even more important, "inner" senses, sensations of the rest of the body, are also received here, such as blood pressure, venous pressure, lung expansion, blood chemical concentrations, and many others.

Also located in the reticular formation are the centers for the control of blood pressure, respiration, heart rate, and other automatic functions. The independent functioning of these centers is obvious; witness the comatose victim of an auto accident whose cortex may be "dead" but who continues to perform the vegetative functions of breathing and control of blood flow.

The reticular system contains areas which excite or inhibit other nervous centers. This system acts in a geneal way to arouse the rest of the brain. It makes no judgment as to the significance of the stimulus. In a normal person this arousal would simply intensify a particular feeling-sensation. When the reticular system is aroused in neurotics, inhibition of a particular feeling may diminish sensory modalities. We often do not feel our hurts during a panic situation such as a fire because our system is galvanized toward the external situation and not our inner one.

The reticular system receives tremendous amounts of information. Through pathways to higher brain centers it both modifies and is modified by the rest of the brain. It controls vegetative functions, helps adjust endocrine secretion, limits sensory input, and affects learning and consciousness. It is stimulated in a non-specific way by all of the sensory systems of the body. Because of its activating functions it is a major source of nervous activity.

The Hypothalamus

The thalamus is the relay center for sensory input to the cortex. The hypothalamus is situated, as its name suggests, below the thalamus. In contrast to the thalamus, it has many functions and contains centers for control of feeding, satiety, thirst, sex, and, through pituitary control, the body's hormone production. It is mainly through the hypothalamus that the limbic circuits direct their energy on the body, producing psychosomatic diseases. Dysfunctions of the hypothalamus affect everything from how much milk a new mother will have available for nursing to how tall she will grow.

It is important to note the relative independence of the hypothalamus from the neocortex—there is little evidence to support any direct connection between the two.

The mediator between the two structures, and situated physically in that position, is the complex "old cortex," or limbic system. The paucity of direct neural communication between the hypothalamus and the neocortex is enormously significant because it indicates there can be endocrine activity in the body without much conscious (cortical) control. Conversely, there can be cortical activity such as ideas, beliefs, and delusions without a direct link to the feelings which gave rise to them. It is the limbic system which keeps them apart.

The Limbic System

The limbic system consists of a rim of cortical tissue at the base of each cerebral (neocortical) hemisphere, overlying the structures discussed above. It is the oldest part of the cortex of man, changing very little in all of human evolution. It has a similar degree of development in all mammals, the only difference being the amount of cortex piled on top of it. Limbic functions and structures are complex and extensive, occupying great areas of the brain, and they deal mainly with emotion and memory. It is, in the Primal sense, *the mediator for mental illness*, because it is the key inhibiting agent of feelings.

The greater the overload of stored pain, the more severe the mental illness. In other words, the greater the amount of painful impulses created through inhibition, the greater the pressure impinging on consciousness. But the amount of underlying Primal Pain depends on the "charge" value of each pain added together. Rape by one's father is a shattering and overwhelming pain, driving the person into deep symbolism (psychosis). Being forced to go to church is a lesser pain. Nevertheless, no matter what the valence of the pain, it is *actively* stored by the memory process in the limbic (temporal) cortex.

The importance of the limbic system in the pain storage process is underlined by Smythies: "The great limbic circuits form the means of evaluating and integrating experience, and finally laying down what is important in the permanent memory store. The amygdala [a key limbic structure] seems concerned mainly with the emotional and motivational aspects of this control system, and the hippocampus with the actual laying down of memory." [8]

The ontologic function of the limbic structure, whether housed in the cat, wolf, or man, is protective. When viewed in this teleologic way, its complexity becomes more comprehensible. It keeps man from his pain, and also keeps him neurotic.

Biologic rhythms of sleep, temperature, excretion, and sexual behavior are also controlled limbically. It is no wonder that when a split occurs between an early Primal feeling and the cortex, the behavior which ensues may be sexual. This can happen because *Primal memories lie below the split and have access to any of the limbic functions without discrimination by the neocortex.* What limbic functions will become involved depend on the life circumstance of the person. He may turn to overeating just as easily as to sex.

Examples

A young girl is not allowed to swear or date boys and is taught in subtle ways that sex is dirty. Further, she learns that God punishes evil minds. Sooner or later, her sex urge may be diminished. Sex thoughts will not enter her mind because such thoughts produce fear and pain. The drive is there because, I am firmly convinced, in healthy bodies drives such as sex are almost equally strong in everyone. What enters her mind? The thought of food, perhaps, but something that is allowable. The various bodily drives then are funneled into eating, and eating becomes compulsive and voracious because the energy of the drive is made up of repressed sexual energy plus all the other repressed needs and feelings. A normal person who is connected internally, who is not suffering from limbic inhibition, could not eat more than he needs. He has no reservoir of pain to drive him to do anything in excess. The same energy source that causes excess eating could just as well result in other kinds of excesses. If the person grows up in a religious household, prayer may become compulsive.

The Primal pressure (of unresolved pains) which lies

[8] T. Smythies, *Neurological Foundations of Psychiatry* (New York: Academic Press, 1966), p. 131.

below cortical access ramifies in many automatic physiologic ways. For example, the same pain which drives sexual thoughts into submersion may also produce vaginismus, a constricted vagina which makes intercourse painful and sometimes impossible. Neurosis is not just mental. There is not only a split brain, but a body split from its feelings—the body "sides" with unconscious feelings.

The same Primal pressure can be channeled off into whatever spillways constitute the weakest link in terms of the person's constitutional makeup. He can develop tics or stammering which are as compelling, and therefore as compulsive, as any other neurotic activity such as sex or eating. The person is helpless before this compulsion even though what he is doing appears to be voluntary.

Here we see the differentiation between psychosis and neurosis. Neurosis is a lower generalization from the pain —there is less pain impulse to be rechanneled via the memory associations. Psychosis is obviously a highly generalized (discussed in detail later) state in which rechanneling is stronger, more diverse, and symbolic. An example of this is a psychotic patient who was terrified of all men and completely unable to look any man in the eye. She was responding to the repressed memory of the look in her father's eyes when he raped her. Later, even pictures of men's eyes frightened her. The rechannelization and symbolization became more remote.

Repression resulting from pain produces a generalized drive state which must be symbolically (neurotically) released because direct connections to real feelings in the neocortex constitute more pain than can be integrated. In this way, the person remains split and forever doomed to act out for a lifetime in his accustomed groove of neurosis.

3. THE NATURE OF PAIN

Pain's Many Forms

We can be hurt in many ways. There are pains which occur even before consciousness is fully developed. Those are not conceptual hurts; they are biologic, but they are stored, nevertheless. For example, a child whose needs for touch and caressing are not met very early in life is being traumatized or overloaded even though he has no consciousness of his needs or their lack of fulfillment. A child forced to toilet-train or to walk before his brain and spinal cord are mature enough is being systematically overloaded. There is evidence that myelinization of nerve sheaths which signifies a readiness to function) is not complete for some twenty years. Forcing a child to run, throw, speak, spell, before the brain is fully ready can be traumatic. And trauma is overload; it is something that cannot be readily integrated in the process of maturation.

Traumas are cumulative. The greater their number the higher the level of residual tension (nonintegrated pain). The greater the level of stored and unresolved pain, the higher the gradient of generalization of response, and the more complex the symbolic behavior. What this means is that with high pain levels, almost anything can set off a neurotic, anxious response. Thus, even remote stimuli are galvanizing. For example, one psychotic patient cringed whenever he heard an automobile horn. He thought it was a signal of "enemy aliens" coming to get him.

Overload

One of the important aspects of cortical myelinization is the relatively late completion of this process in the neocortical tissue of the frontal lobe. This part of the brain is concerned with abstraction and generalization. The completion of this process does not take place until the age of five or six. It is then that the child can be hurt conceptually; meanings can hurt him and can be catastrophic. Until this time, the child may suffer any number of insults, humiliations, and abuses, but will respond to each stimulus as a thing unto itself. If the event is traumatic enough in itself (rape, for example), then the pain will produce a disconnection at that time. But that is not the usual case. Rather, not letting a child be himself happens insidiously, a bit at a time. He is spanked when he soils himself, told to drink his milk whether he wants it or not, told how to hold his fork, scolded when he runs naked in the street, and so on. And one day when the brain can generalize all those previously disparate experiences, the weight of them all congealed in a meaning—"They hate me, the real me"—overloads the child's capacity to integrate and he fragments. He does not fully feel the previously fragmented state and becomes stimulus-bound. That is, he again treats experience as discrete, nonconnected entities. He must do so to survive and keep great pain away.

So it is the meaning which is catastrophic, the meaning we became capable of feeling at the age of five. Meaning *is* a generalization. It is the accumulated valence of all those previous assaults. This is why so many of us become effectively neurotic at about the age of five or six. To return to a fragmented existence is to avoid meaning. And, tragically, the person grows up searching for meaning in every place but the right one.

I want to stress that the valence of any single experience can be sufficient to produce disconnection even before myelinization. Traumatic births set up a tension in the system because the experience could not be integrated on *any* level. Situations in the crib can do the same, such as extremely rough, tense handling or insufficient handling.

There are many ways to overload the system, some quite subtle. One patient was overhandled, tweaked, pushed, and not left alone by doting grandparents. At the age of eight months, she could no longer tolerate the overstimulation, and having no way to shut it off, she began seizure activity. During a Primal, she relived the pain of the overstimulation, pain too great to be consciously integrated as an infant.

Overload can derive from too much touch, from not enough touch, or from a *meaning* derived from a single experience which, though not intrinsically traumatic in and of itself, becomes the last straw which produces disintegration. Not everyone has a seizure under overload. There are many ways to become unconscious. Some patients just become numb and dumb.

What patients report about birth Primals is significant. They say that they "know" somewhere on top what they are going through while they are having a birth Primal, yet feel powerless to stop what they sense is a neurological sequence being run off. It is dramatic evidence of the split consciousness. During the Primal most of their being was engulfed by the infantile experience, but in a conscious way. Prior to the Primal most of their being was engulfed by this very same birth trauma but in an unconscious way; that is, the person suffered inexplicable tension and neurosis. The birth trauma becomes accessible to conscious experience when the person has paved the way with less painful Primals. If the birth was severly traumatic and carries a heavy valence of pain, the system will not be able to integrate that experience until other Pains are out of the way. It is not that one's pain tolerance builds in Primal Therapy; rather, the *overall* load is reduced in steady accretions so that ever greater traumas can be experienced. For example, toward the end of therapy two patients relived the pure pain of surgery, one an abortion and the other an appendectomy. When a drug such as LSD opens the feeling gate, all of the pains of one's life pour into consciousness at once, resulting *not* in specific Primals but in symbolic ideation and/or physical symptoms.

Sometimes it is only after a purely physical Primal that a patient can make sense out of what he has been through. Over a period of days, one patient felt, first, cold buttocks, then cold knees, then cold feet, and finally he blacked out. He had no idea what he was going through until two weeks had passed, then it all fell into place—breech birth. This was subsequently documented by contacting his mother. The overload of that experience caused it to be felt in fragments, until the entire experience could be integrated.

What is becoming clear is that it does not matter whether consciousness was suppressed by a general anesthetic, by lack of myelinization and development of consciousness, or through neurosis. The system registers an overload nevertheless, and produces lifelong tension until that pain is connected and integrated. This can be quite subtle. One previously psychotic patient had a Primal of being strangled by the cord during birth. His experience was a feeling first quite comfortable and then suddenly traumatized. As he came out of the Primal he said that his paranoia (or disposition toward it) started then when he "learned" that his environment was hostile and not to be trusted. This early experience, plus a lifetime with parents who could not be trusted, produced a person who reacted in his adult life on the basis of unconscious memory. He was suspicious and believed that no one could be trusted, and no trusting experience in his adulthood could shake him from his paranoid ideation.

The major Primal Scene is the time when a child puts it all together, or at least starts to do so. But the pain of the meaning of all his previous experiences becomes an overload to the system, producing a "blowout" or symptom. The symptom may be stuttering, learning difficulties, a tic; the symptom is the spillway to handle excess pain. The notion of overload is discussed in a book on brain function and learning disabilities:

> A number of children manifest disturbances only when more than one process is required at a given time. It is in this context that the concept of overloading takes on value. . . . A dysfunction in the brain lowers the tolerance limits for processing information. A child [may] show symptoms of disintegration when interneurosensory and complex integrative functions are required; he then manifests poor recall, random movements, poor attention, disinhibition and, in rare instances, seizures. Overloading can cause a generalized breakdown in the neurological processes which has implications not only for reducing the ability to learn but for total well-being, including medical treatment and management.[9]

What I believe happens at the Primal Scene is that all those previous rejections and being left alone begin to flood the organism at once as they pertain to the Primal feeling. The organism cannot handle such a flooding and does pretty much what Johnson and Myklebust say it does—random movements, poor attention, and so on. In

[9] D. Johnson and H. R. Myklebust, *Learning Disabilities* (New York: Grune and Stratton, 1967), p. 31.

order to rid itself of the overload, the neurotic organism must slowly integrate bits of the feelings with its memories.

The "Gate" Theory

The "gate" theory of Melzack and Casey helps us understand the overload process neurologically:

> Cells in the medial brainstem are capable of summation of input from spatially separate body sites . . . so that [this] information is transformed into intensity information . . . a critical intensity level activates those brain areas subserving positive affect and approach tendency. Beyond that level, the output activates areas underlying negative affect and aversive drive. We propose, therefore, that the drive mechanisms associated with pain are activated when the somatosensory input into the motivational-affective system exceeds the critical level.[10]

In summary, too much intensive input means pain, the gate then shuts off more input, and the person is driven to avoid the situation.

What is even more significant is that *the critical level of intensity is regulated by the limbic system. Animals seek low-intensity stimulation of limbic structures, but "avoid or actively try to stop high intensity stimulation of the same areas."* [11]

This relates to Primal theory because it is not a single event such as rejection by a friend that floods us with pain. Rather, the single event is shut off and/or avoided because it arouses a *flood* of old impulses regarding rejection. To feel one rejection directly, then, would mean to open the gate to the total Primal feeling. We keep Primal feeling away by shutting off any triggering feeling or event. We cannot feel a single "nontraumatic" rejection because of what it can open up.

[10] R. Malzack and K. L. Casey, "The Affective Dimension of Pain," in *Feelings and Emotions,* ed. by Magda Arnold (New York: Academic Press, 1970), p. 61.

[11] *Ibid.*

The notion of a gate which shuts down too much pain has found application in a process known as electroanalgesia. It is used in cases of chronic intractable pain. It involves the use of electronic stimulators implanted in the region of the dorsal column of the spinal cord. Electroanalgesia is based on the hypothesis that there are specialized afferent fibers which inhibit pain messages when stimulated, so a jolt of the implant by a pocket transmitter sets off a flood of inhibitory impulses. The paramedial ascending system

> first penetrates the ancient limbic forebrain, and then makes contacts throughout the paleomammaliam brain [limbic system], man's inheritance from lower mammals. Here, in regions taken up by visceral sensations, there are thoughts and feelings—but none expressible directly in verbal terms. Here also . . . lie the slender nerve threads and pencil-thick tracts which form the control system for influencing pain perception at both spinal levels and in the ascending fibers.[12]

What the above indicates once again is the suppressing function on pain of the limbic system. The gate theory is controversial, and there are a number of interpretations as to why pain becomes repressed and unfelt. Rather than positing the existence of specific ascending inhibitory nerve tracts, one wonders if the flooding process alone— the mass bombardment of simultaneous stimuli—is sufficient to set off the inhibitory processes of the hippocampal gate, hence producing no feeling. Because the organism cannot assimilate a flood of impulses, it shuts them all out. Those impulses, taken singly, may not be intrinsically painful, but when massed with many impulses they become transformed into pain. Thus, in a neat dialectic, too much feeling becomes transmuted into its opposite—no feeling.

This, of course, is the Primal contention—events in our early lives set off too much feeling, in general. A person could take one reprimand or one humiliation, but too

[12] "Pain," *Medical World News* (Dec. 11, 1970), pp. 20–32.

many of those cause him to split away from his feeling self. A psychologically "dead" person is not one with few feelings but rather someone with great amounts of repressed feeling. A person who kills without remorse is not nonfeeling (it takes tremendous feeling to kill); he is someone overloaded with feeling, hence shut down and unable to show any feeling, remorse or otherwise.

Perhaps we can now understand the so-called paradoxical reaction of drugs—why, for example, hyperactive children are given massive doses of stimulants such as amphetamines to calm them down. The overload aids in their repressive process—something they could not do on their own. It also explains why epileptic children are given heavy doses of amphetamine to stop their seizures.

Corroborative evidence concerning the limbic system and its pain-suppressive functions comes from the work of Heath at Tulane University School of Medicine. Electrodes were chronically implanted in the brains of several dozen individuals. These subjects were usually in intractable pain. Heath's patients experienced symptomatic relief through intracranial self-stimulation of limbic areas. The reported consequences of limbic activation were: elimination or depression and anxiety, immediate relief of pain, and increased alertness.[13]

Melzack, in discussing the general question of pain, asserts, "Painful stimuli produce long-lasting changes—that is, pain 'memories' in the nervous system. . . . Behavorial and clinical evidence indicates that memory—including the persisting influences of the individual's personality—must be taken into account [to understand the persistence of pain]." [14]

The evidence indicates that early memory is blocked in many neurotics because each memory fits into the painful matrix. To remember one event is to release more pain. Conversely, to release the pain is to unleash a myriad of memories. There is little neurologic reason for the repression of early memory, since the cortex involved with memory becomes myelinated early in our development. We

[13] R. G. Heath (ed.), *The Role of Pleasure in Behavior* (New York: Hoeber, 1964).

[14] Melzack and Casey, *op. cit.*, p. 29.

should be able to remember events even though we could not conceptualize the memory.

If we clearly understand that disparate memories are shielded from consciousness because of pain, then when pain is felt, relationships are understood, memories explode, and concepts flow out of the organism to make comprehensible widely disparate events in a person's life. It is then that he can easily go back and remember events in the crib and playpen. He will become profoundly insightful because it was buried feelings which drove neurotic behaviors and made him unaware of his motivations. Feeling helps make it all make sense.

Let us no take a closer and more detailed look at those brain structures which mediate repression, or "disconnection."

4. THE BASIS AND DESCRIPTION OF THE DISCONNECTION

The Hippocampus and Memory Blockage

We have discussed the nature and storage of painful memories and the function of lower brain centers. We are aware that neurosis results from the splitting of early pains from conscious awareness. It has been suggested that the disconnection occurs within the limbic system, and there is evidence to suggest that the hippocampus is of prime importance in this respect.

The hippocampus is a limbic structure underlying the temporal cortex; it winds posteriorly and forward again to finally terminate via various pathways below the cortical gray tissue of the frontal lobe. It literally runs from limbic cortex to neocortex. Much of what we know of its function comes from data concerning seizure disorders, such as psychomotor epilepsy.

A dramatic statement of the importance of the hippocampus, based on studies of hippocampal seizures in animals, was made by Gellhorn: "The most striking demonstration of the neural integration of limbic structures and the potential *dichotomy in function of the limbic and neocortical systems* is provided by mapping the spread of an afterdischarge induced by electrical stimulation of the hippocampus. Such discharges have the tendency to spread throughout and to be largely confined to the limbic system." [15] This discharge renders the limbic system ineffective, and studies of these animals help assess the effects of limbic deprivation. It is interesting to note that these animals exhibit a loss of response to stimuli and psedocatatonic activity suggestive of schizophrenia. The limbic system can be either partially or totally blocked. The extent of blockage determines the amount of symbolic behavior—hence the severity of the neurosis or psychosis.

Webster and Voneida produced lesions in the feline hippocampus and found that cats could still learn tasks but could not *unlearn* previously learned ones. Though they punished the cats by withholding food, the cats continued to perform old tasks to get food. They concluded that the hippocampus was necessary to extinguish previously learned behavior—*to repress the past.*[16]

Understanding hippocampal function is central to a comprehension of the nature of the neurotic split. Recent research involving chlorpromazine, provides interresting suggestions as to the nature of a process which many psychiatrists since Freud have considered almost occult. When sensory input arouses the neocortex in nondrug states, it produces a "desychronized" pattern of brain-wave activity (this is in contradistinction to the sychronous pattern which is characteristic of sleep). Another pattern characterizes this arousal in the hippocampus—a theta rhythm—and the theta rhythm is closely associated with the desychronized arousal pattern of the cortex.

It has been suggested that the theta rhythm is an expression of *activation* occuring in the hippocampus.[17] This means that inhibition of nerve impulses (or repression of feeling-laden memory) is an *active process*. In other

[15] Gellhorn, *op. cit.*, citing B. R. Kaada, p. 86.
[16] D. Webster and T. J. Voneida, *Experimental Neurology* (New York: Academic Press, 1964), p. 170.
[17] C. Pfeiffer and J. R. Smythies, *International Review of Neurobiology* (New York: Academic Press, 1965), pp. 79, 84.

words, some nerves and their synapses function to transmit impulses, while others function to block or inhibit transmission. There is much evidence to indicate that there is a great concentration of inhibitory synapses in the hippocampus. *The hippocampus, then can be considered a significant brain structure involved in inhibition —in repression of feeling impulses.* Because its function is to keep old memories away from consciousness, it is a key structure in the formation of mental illness.

Let us look now at the effects of LSD and chlorpromazine on neocortical and hippocampal EEG patterns. We shall have to keep in mind that some research is contradictory in relation to these patterns. Further, in discussing the effects of drugs on EEG patterns I do not suggest a necessary direct-line action of the drugs on the structure described. Changes in the hippocampal pattern may well be the result of the drug elsewhere, and there is a circuit from both the frontal cortex and the reticular system (mediated by the septum) that is responsible for this rhythm. Nevertheless, for the moment I want to concentrate on the function of the theta rhythm and not on the locus of its initiation.

Chlorpromazine sychronizes neocortical EEG patterns and inhibits the theta rhythm. In short, it produces a sleep-type pattern in the cortex, and with the cortex "less feeling," less inhibition seems to be occuring in the hippocampus. This suggests that part of the impetus for hippocampal activation (or inhibition) is derived from cortical activity. LSD acts to produce a flattening of the theta rhythm associated with a desychronized (aroused) cortex. This would mean that at the time of greatest excitement in the person on an LSD trip, part of his brain, the hippocampus, is actually functioning *less*.[18] The theta rhythm has disappeared; unchallenged feelings and memories, ordinarily blocked by inhibitory synapses in the hippocampus, are passing through the limbic system toward cortical or conscious awareness. In street slang, the person is on a "bummer." His real feelings are magnified. The frontal cortex is forced to feel or inhibit. The latter

[18] The ability of the limbic system to repress pain is enhanced by its rich supply of serotonin, an inhibitory agent.

has become impossible with LSD, and so the pain arrives unchallenged if the dose is great enough. Because of the flooding of Primal Pain produced by the "open gate," the cortex is forced into more strained defenses such as psychotic ideation and/or psychedelic reactions. The cortex has nowhere to run for help except further into itself. To summarize the LSD experience: because of the defunctionalized hippocampus and the inhibition of cortial control—the blocking of neuronal transmission at the synaptic level—the neocortex is unable to effectively inhibit so that defenses become either entirely neocortical (such as hallucinations) or the feeling is felt (a Primal experience).

Electrophysiologic evidence for the inhibitory function of the hippocampus is found in Torda's work.[19] She found that dreams are reported when hippocampal theta activity is between two to four cycles per second, and not reported at higher frequencies. Because dream activity is an index of the ascent of feelings (see section on Dreams), this would mean that we are more accessible to our feelings when the hippocampus is less active. During the slow theta phase, feelings begin their journey to consciousness, where, in neurotics, they are wrapped in symbolization for safekeeping. We see this by the increase in cortical activity (as measured on the EEG) when the hippocampus is temporarily less active.

In dream sleep, wave amplitude rises; this may indicate that a greater number of neurons have been recruited to keep feelings from becoming a totally conscious, connected Primal experience.[20] Without such compensation for the slowdown in wave frequency, we all might be having Primals during our sleep.

Stimulants such as amphetamines increase hippocampal theta action. I would assume that this is because the stim-

---

[19] Clara Torda, "Observations on a Physiological Process Related to Dreams," in *Communications in Behavioral Biology* (New York: Academic Press, 1968), Part A, 2, pp. 39–45.

[20] I do not wish to oversimplify amplitude. It is more than simply the number of neurons recruited. The matter of synchrony must be taken into account, as well.

ulant heightens the possibilities for feelings, requiring more inhibition—the result: little or no dreaming. What we are seeing is how important that structure is in repression and, more important, the relationship of repression to other factors including dream life. A relaxed brain seems to be one with slow theta action; a feeling person, in short, is one who does not have a brain galvanized for defense. We need much more research on theta, but we may be beginning to have some objective brain-wave correlates for what is a true feeling person—a well or healthy human being.

By careful spectral analysis of waves we may be able to chart the course of therapeutic progress.

By careful analysis of all the brain-wave data, we may be able to quantify the degree of repression in a neurotic; how good is his prognosis, length of therapeutic time required, and so on.

By correlating all this EEG data with our other measures such as blood pressure, eletromyograph, body temperature, etc., we may be able to produce a composite picture of a person's total psychophysiologic state.

Chlorpromazine depresses reticular stimulation, which again has an effect on the hippocampus. Electrical stimulation of the reticular structure in rats, for example, which ordinarily produced disorganized or "neurotic" behavior, did not do so when they were given tranquilizers such as chlorpromazine.[21] We can begin to see how complex drug action affects the brain because brain structures are interrelated and depression of one structure may cause stimulation of another or vice versa.[22]

[21] See C. Kornetsky and M. Eliasson, "Reticular Stimulation and Chlorpromazine: Animal Model for Schizophrenic Overarousal," *Science*, Vol. 165 (1969), pp. 1273–1274.

[22] I have omitted much of the research on the amygdala, a limbic structure closely associated with the hippocampus. Preston believes that the amygdala is a funnel for inhibitory impulses impinging on the brainstem, particularly the hypothalamus. See J. B. Preston, "Effects of Chlorpromazine on the Nervous System of the Cat: A Possible Neural Basis for Action." Annual Meeting, New York, Eastern Associates of Electroencephalographers (December 7, 1955). There is increased electrical activity in the amygdala of cats following

5. THE PERMANENCE OF PRIMAL PAIN

Reverberating Circuits

What is the neurophysiologic correlate of inhibited Primal Pain? It would seem to be a self-perpetuating nerve cycle traveling in a loop of neurons below the level of consciousness. These memories are like encapsulated messages circulating in perpetuity around the brain. Gerard discusses this process: "Perhaps, then, a memory is a *continuing activity*—a trapped message running round and round a particular set of loops formed by neurons synapsing [connecting] on one another." [23] These patterns are called "reverberating circuits." I would surmise that proper connections of Primal memories to the cortex are shunted away from connecting at the synapse or junction point between nerve cells.

By alteration of the chemistry at the synapse, certain messages get blocked and certain others are facilitated in their travel. Once a painful memory impulse gets shunted into symbolic channels, a "groove" develops—nerve pathways become habituated. This has been worked out neurochemically by Mcgaugh and Petrinovich,[24] who state:

> Increased activity in neurons increases the amount of transmitter substance released by the cells. The increased utilization of transmitter substance causes an increase (enzyme induction) of the enzymes involved

---

injection of chlorpromazine, suggesting that the drug stimulates inhibitory activity. Similarly, electrical stimulation of the amygdala in cats resulted in amnesia. (See B. R. Kaada's work.) Penfield stimulated the amygdaloid complex of humans undergoing surgery and concluded also that this structure exerted a widespread inhibitory influence on the central nervous system. We see, again, how crucial is the entire limbic system in severing memory and suppressing feelings.

[23] R. W. Gerard, "The Brain Mechanism of the Mind," in *An Outline of Man's Knowledge*, ed. by L. Brys (New York: Doubleday, 1960). Italics added.

[24] J. L. Mcgaugh and L. F. Petrinovich, "Effects of Drugs on Learning and Memory," in *International Review of Neurobiology* (New York: Academic Press, 1965), p. 101.

in the manufacture of transmitter substance. This, in turn, would lead to far-reaching intracellular changes. Thus it becomes clear that an increased amount of transmitter substance released by any axon following repeated stimulation could be the major factor in establishing and maintaining the particular mechanisms of memory.

This suggests that memory is a facilitated circuit which becomes more "grooved" because of constant use. Constant use produces more transmitter substance (enzymes), which makes the circuit more likely to be used again. Here we see why a circuit becomes reinforced and an impulse becomes reverberating, why defenses become stabilized, and why certain modes of thought become fixated and unchanged by later learning. When a child is not allowed to think "hate" or "sex," the pressure of those feelings becomes diverted into other more acceptable channels of thought, and those permissible channels become reinforced simply out of use. This is how we stay symbolic and neurotic, how we suffer from intractable compulsions, and how even certain facial expressions ("Smile! For chrissakes, put on a happy face!") which are permissible and demanded become habituated.

There is evidence that interacting nerve cells grow toward one another in a process call neurobiotaxis. Hebb discusses this process in depth.[25] Knobs begin to grow on neurons, expanding their area of contact with other nerve cells so that messages are facilitated. We could conjecture that a feeling shunted away from proper connection by enzyme induction finally "grows" toward its misconnection.

Being neurotic, then, is physical fact in the brain. If neurotic behavior is literally circuitous behavior, then being straight means just that in the brain. What makes circumlocutions necessary, I submit, is blocked straightness"—because being straight means pain. Thus, a person

[25] D. O. Hebb, "The Possibility of a Dual Trace Mechanism," in *Readings in Physiological Psychology*, ed. by Landauer (New York: McGraw-Hill, 1967), pp. 476–479.

may become oversexed around women because he cannot feel his mother's rejection—he is acting out *against* the feeling of rejection by getting women's love. During therapy, on more than one occasion, we have seen a male patient cry for his mother until the pain was so great that he had to block it, and he then immediately had an erection.

M. W. Gordon discusses neuronal (nerve) facilition and points out that when memory is solidified, there is a new synthesis of protein at the synapse, "imposing permanent modifications which resist disruption." [26] The rate of protein synthesis is directly related to the rate of neuronal activity, according to Gordon, so that the structure of the synapse itself changes in terms of how much it is stimulated. He indicates that "use relates different synaptic endings one to another." [27] He goes on to say, "A facilitation of a given pathway can influence a neuronal network so complex that *almost any connection may develop*." [28] He indicates that bizarre and nonadaptive behavior can result from any stimulus because of this multiplicity of possibilities of neuronal connections.

Gordon further states that affective states (feelings) profoundly affect the time required to fix a memory—to convert it from short term to long term. Animals taught to perform a task while receiving a small shock "fixed" memory in two minutes, whereas those who received no shock took thirty minutes to convert a short-term memory to a long-term one. He theorizes that affect (feeling or emotion) influences the amount of electrical stimulation of the brain and that this "alerting" influence probably increases the rate of synaptic discharge, thus producing the required quantitative change in a short time. One wonders if the same thing could be said for highly charged Primal Scenes where there is massive stimulation of the brain resulting in "fixed" reverberating memory patterns.

[26] M. W. Gordon, "Neuronal Plasticity and Memory," *American Journal of Orthopsychiatry*, Vol. 39, No. 4 (July, 1969), p. 587.
[27] *Ibid.*, p. 590.
[28] *Ibid.* Italics added.

The notion of trapped reverberating Primal memories is significant in the present context, for if there were no such below-conscious forces shaping our perceptions, actions, and reactions, there would be no neurotic life styles and no neurotic personalities.[29] There would be no continuous and unconscious hunching of the shoulders, no chronic facial set, no same whiny, highpitched voice or constant automatic grinding of the teeth during sleep. Life circumstances push each of us in a different direction in order to defend against the pains. Those directions are the *forms* of neurosis, whether homosexuality, criminality, addiction.

But these forms are not to be confused with disease entities. For example, there are no disease entities called "addiction" or "alcoholism." These are but the names of the medicines for pain. Some of us take a direct route to kill the pain; others wend their way through academia and obtain a Ph.D. to do it. The forms of defense depend on what is available to us in our environment, but they are still offshoots from relatively few underlying Primal feelings, quite similar in all of us. The Ph.D. and the criminal have simply taken different routes. The substrata of pain below the diverse forms of neurosis explain why so many different ailments ranging from ulcers to hallucinations are all treated with the same kind of drugs —pain killers and tranquilizers. These agents block the Primal generating sources.

If there were no Primal Pool of feelings, there would be no recurrent dream with almost the same content for twenty or thirty years. It is a sign that something needs to be resolved. The person is stuck and trapped in a feeling which constantly requires that it be shielded from full consciousness. These recurrent dreams are behaviors, just as any daytime thought is behavior. During the daytime there is still the recurrent theme, but we do not call it a dream. The person may have the identical ideas about women, politics, and minorities, irrespective of his experience, for years. These ideas are, again, the symbols shield-

[29] To repeat: Memory need not have been something conscious. The organism "remembers" or registers its unresolved traumas, such as at birth, with very little consciousness needed at all.

ing him from the Pain. He clings to these ideas no matter what his experience tells him, just as he has his recurrent dream no matter how hard he tries to shake it.

To see that a recurrent dream is part of the general symbolic behavior of neurotics is to understand the nature of all neurosis. Neurosis *is* compulsive behavior (we are compelled to hold ourselves in the same way each day, to speak the same way, etc.) to cover Pain. The painful feelings don't go away just because it is daylight. The same feelings which are so active in producing recurrent dreams also produce recurrent daytime behavior with the same theme acted out.

Flash-card research suggests the existence of reverberating circuits. Words are flashed to subjects on cards; some of the words are neutral and others are vulgar and obscene. Many subjects not only take much longer to perceive the cards with the vulgar words but in some cases do not see them at all. What this means is that their perceptions are organized below the level of consciousness: since they did not know consciously what was on the cards they failed to perceive. Unacceptable perceptions were repressed, obviously, by subconscious forces. The assumption is that proper perception would have produced pain because the words carried some danger about them—the danger of being "dirty" or "crude" and therefore of being unloved. This experiment has something to say about objectivity in general. Clearly, what we see and even *if* we see depends on underlying circuits which may block correct perception of reality. How a jury votes on an obscenity case may have no less to do with the objective facts presented and much more on whether the systems of its members can absorb these facts.

Another experiment using flash cards had only neutral words on them such as "cow" or "hay." With each presentation of the card the subject was given a mild electric shock, so mild that he was unaware of it. Later, the same cards were presented without the shock. The person still showed the skin changes that were evident when he was shocked. In other words, the body reacts to pain even when the pain is not consciously recognized, and can be conditioned to react as though in pain even when the painful stimulus no longer exists. The organism reacts on the basis of *subconscious memory* in automatic fashion. As Gerard indicates,

> Messages reach an appropriate region of the brain and lead to partial and incomplete consequences. Perhaps, here also some reverberation of messages around neuron loops and nets is needed for full response. If the incoming message starts to reverberate but is cut off too soon, full awareness does not develop. And the cutoff could come in many ways—by the setting up of suppressing or inhibiting messages that feed back to the incoming path and block it, for example, or by failure of facilitating impulses.[30]

Gerard seems to confirm this Primal point: A message of major but painful import begins its reverberations but never achieves *full* consciousness. It is, instead, fully organized below consciousness in the same way that not being able to see vulgar words on flash cards is organized. At some point in the young child's life the Primal message was understood for a brief flash but soon repressed before its full impact could be felt.

Himwich and associates have stated the following regarding reverberating circuits:

> Papez suggested that some structures of the temporal lobe may be regarded as a unified system functioning as a reverberating circuit or feedback mechanism. When the hippocampus is stimulated it gives rise to impulses which initiate the Papez circuit. These impulses are transmitted from the hippocampus through the fornix, to the mammilary bodies of the hypothalamus. From that area they continue to the anterior thalamic nuclei and attain the cortex of the brain by way of the cingulate gryus. *By means of the Papez circuit the reactions of structures especially adapted for emotional activities attain awareness.* Though each of the member structures of the reverberating circuit makes its own contribution, the total effect on behavior is modified and influenced by the activities of the other components

[30] Gerard, *op. cit.*, p. 86.

as well. . . . The amygdaloid nuclei are in functional relationships and indirect anatomic connections with the areas in the Papez circuit.

They go on to discuss the relationship of the limbic and reticular systems: "The limbic areas project to the reticular formation from which they receive afferents in return and in both instances the hypothalamus is synaptically embedded in the descending and ascending loops of this circuit. The functional state of the hypothalamus is thus inseparably related to the neural activity of the limbic systems as well as that of the midbrain circuit." [31]

The chief contributions, from the Primal frame of reference, of this research is the indication that the Papez circuit "serves to bring emotional reactions to the level of awareness," [32] and that the hypothalamus may be continuously stimulated owing to its nodal position in limbic activity. We can see the mediating role of the hypothalamus in psychosomatic illness.

Though a person does not seem to be under stress, the reverberating memories keep him under duress. He may fall prey to disease resulting from distortions of the hormone system even though he has been living in a calm and serene atmosphere. (Please see illustrations for where feelings are blocked in the brain and rechanneled.)

Now let us discuss where the units of memory reside.

6. PRIMAL MEMORY AND BRAIN STRUCTURE: THE PERMANENT RECORDING OF EARLY EXPERIENCE

The Temporal Cortex

Startling information about memory and the limbic system has come from the experiments by neurosurgeon Wilder Penfield.[33] Penfield has performed surgery under

[31] H. W. Himwich, A. Morillo, and W. Steiner, "Drugs Affecting Rinencephalic Structures," *Journal of Neuropsychiatry* (Aug., 1962), pp. s17–s19.

[32] *Ibid.*, pp. 6–25.

[33] W. Penfield and P. Perot, "The Brain's Record of Audi-

local anesthesia on temporal lobe epileptics. With the patient's skull flap open during surgery, Penfield found that by stimulating sections of the temporal cortex with an electrode he could evoke old memories. These memories ran off in the exact sequence in which they occurred and were quite vivid. The patient continued to describe the memory as long as the electrode remained in place and stopped as soon as the electrode was withdrawn. When the electrode probe was placed near a memory site, a hallucination was experienced. When it was brought back to the original site, the same memory occurred again and was experienced in the same temporal order as before.

The memory always began at the beginning. Penfield described one case in which a probe was placed near a memory site; what occured was a hallucination: "There seem to be robbers nearby." When the probe was again placed at the memory site, the memory was: "I can remember my brother holding a gun on me." This was evidently the central pain. The further the probe was placed from the central pain, the greater the symbolism. Symbolic behavior, then, *may be literally a function of the distance from the site of feeling.*

In discussing hallucinations which often precede an epileptic fit, Penfield, in a separate study, stated, "They are reproductions of past experience." [34] They are, to use the Primal framework, symbolic derivatives of real memories. This concept of symbols, such as hallucinations or delusions, being reproductions of the past is important because it gives us an insight into dream symbols as well. When a current event triggers off an old memory (in much the same way as Penfield's electrode did), instead of the memory arising to be felt and resolved, symbols are experienced in its place. In the case of epilepsy, there is a convulsive fit. The aura and the hallucination just before the fit suggest that an old feeling is close, is symbolized "psychologically" (because of the strength of the repressed feeling), and the body convulses from the mas-

---

tory and Visual Experience," *Brain*, Vol. 86, Part 4 (1963), pp. 596–695. See also Penfield and Krustiansen, *Epileptic Seizure* (Springfield, Ill.: Charles Thomas Co., 1951).

[34] Penfield and Perot, *op. cit.*, p. 686.

sive discharge of that previously disconnected ascending force.[35]

The epileptic symptom, like any symptom, takes the place of the connected experience of pain. It occurs because the exact memory and its feeling could not safely be conjoined. Epilepsy is the random physical discharge of tension; psychosis is the psychologic one. Psychogenic epilepsy (and it is the psychogenic symptom I am discussing) stands equal to symbolic dreams in that both occur when proper connections cannot be made.

Sometimes, in Penfield's experiments, placing an electrode on a certain memory site during surgery would make the person feel as though he were going to have an attack. But there were no attacks, and rarely was there deep emotional pain with these scenes. Penfield described the experience with a seventeen-year-old epileptic during surgery. Many of his attacks were initiated by listening to jaz. Associated with the beginnings of an attack was a vague memory of trying to reach out for something. When a certain point of the temporal cortex was stimulated, the boy said, "I feel like I'm going to have an attack." When the probe was moved a bit forward, he said, "I feel as though I am in a bathroom at school . . . sort of a flashback." He said, "I seemed to be there." [36]

These descriptions leave one to wonder what the true effect of the school bathroom scene was, and if possibly there were elements of the memory which could not be evoked because they were locked away with the painful feeling. In other words, even with an electric probe it is possible that the affective elements of a memory are not brought up in order to keep Primals under control. We should note here that even when memories would seem to have severe affect, the person being probed does not seem to show it in any deep way. (One example Penfield gave was a memory such as, "Everyone is yelling at me. Make them stop!"—said with little feeling.) But in reality this phenomenon is little different from what happens in some conventional therapies when a person will have a

[35] Wayne Barker discusses the exact process in full in his book *Brain Storms* (New York: Grove Press, 1968).

[36] Penfield and Perot, *op. cit.*, p. 651.

memory with little affect (because he is disconnected) and later in Primal Therapy may be convulsed by it because he *is* connected.

Further evidence regarding the notion of disconnection even under electrode probing is suggested, for in no case reported by Penfield did the person actually relive the scene. He "saw" the scene and related what he saw (and what he heard) to the doctor. In other words, the patient was dissociated from the true affect of the scene. To let go of the present and sink into that memory, talking to the people in it, might then have produced a far different result from what Penfield reported.

Penfield goes on to discuss the electrode probing in relation to the temporal cortex:

> The fact that application of a gentle electrical current on certain portions of the temporal cortex can switch on the recording suggests that the engram [memory trace] is, in fact, a permanent and continuous thread of facilitation. Facilitation lowers the threshold of resistance to the passage of nerve impulses. This should not suggest to us that the engram and its thread of facilitation are localized in the temporal cortex beneath the surgeon's electrode. Indeed, it suggests only that there is a scanning mechanism, in the temporal cortex, that is capable of activating the thread of facilitation at a distance.[37]

The reason that the whole "memory" or reverberating circuit cannot be localized within a small section of the cortex is obvious. A painful Primal memory concerning "mother" would involve connections to disparate parts of the neocortex. A mental picture (occipital lobe), touch (parietal), smell (frontal), sound (temporal), all have contributions to make to the intricate circuit; and no less important is the word "mother" itself, stored in the parietal cortex. Primal circuits may be triggered by reproducing any one or more of the sensory modalities comprising the memory of mother—which is why we insist

[37] W. Penfield, "Engrams in the Human Brain," Royal Society of Medicine, *Proceedings*, Vol. 61 (Aug., 1968), pp. 839–840.

that patients bring with them to therapy their early photo albums.

Penfield calls the temporal cortex the "interpretive cortex" because it is "part of an automatic mechanism that scans the record of the past. It makes *subconscious* automatic judgments that have to do with the individual and his environment." [38]

Let us see what this really means in terms of neurosis and its cure. In a primal group recently, I had a woman suddenly embrace a homosexual man who was suffering at that moment from what he described as a "vague hurt." He had already had a minor Primal earlier. With the embrace he immediately broke down and experienced the wracking pain associated with never having been touched and caressed by his mother. This complex circuit was so painful that he automatically and unconsciously avoided contact with women in order to circumvent the pain. The sudden embrace by a woman at a time when he was vulnerable plugged into the reverberating circuit of pain. The scanner, through the modality of touch, activated a flood of impulses—a flood of years of deprivation and need. These impulses then must either be blocked (as he had always done) or be felt. The way that he had automatically deflected the pain was by avoidance of women (by homosexuality). Attraction to men was not the motive for his homosexuality; men were the path of least resistance. Without this defense, he experienced the painful feelings. Cure of this patient's homosexuality involved feeling the pain; there was no longer a reason for avoidance of women. Access to those Primal circuits, then, is what makes Primal Therapy curative.

Thus the temporal cortex is a scanning device which translates each new experience on the basis of the memory bank. Each new event is interpreted and acted upon in terms of this latent storehouse (the role of the frontal lobe in this process will be discussed). The temporal scanner selects out of the past similar experiences and then relays the total message, past and present, to other brain centers for processing.

[38] *Ibid.* Italics added.

The fact that pain can be reactivated is exemplified in the phantom-limb phenomenon. This is the experience of continued suffering from the wound of a removed limb. Nathan stimulated a few of the nerves which had previously innervated an old wound in an amputated limb.[39] He found that "once the stimulation was adequate, the *whole pattern* of the previous injury was experienced. There was not merely the jab of pain in the original localization: the entire pattern of sensation with the previous wounding was felt." [40]

As with the hurts of the homosexual discussed above, it doesn't take much to bring up the whole pattern of hurt. Fragments of a stored experience (a sight, sound, or smell) set off the entire neurophysiologic circuit. One implication of this is that as adults we do not need to live with our parents in order to continue to suffer from early childhood experiences. We store the memories in the same way that the phantom limb is stored centrally. It will be as useful to say to a neurotic, "There's nothing to be so upset and nervous about," as it would to tell an amputee not to hurt anymore since his limb is gone.

Short-term and Long-term Primal Memory

We should differentiate Primal memories from other more recent memories. Short-term memories and long-term memories are essentially two different kinds of processes. In certain kinds of brain damage, recent memory is affected in such a way that the person can discuss his childhood with you, walk out of the room for five minutes, and not know who you are when he returns. He can still go on discussing his childhood, however.

Recent evidence (I have cited Gordon's work earlier) indicates that everything that happens to us is not stored immediately. Many neurochemical processes must take place in order for the memory to be set down permanently. If during this storage process certain drugs were given, or if a massive electrical jolt were administered, the

[39] P. W. Nathan, "Pain Traces Left in the Central Nervous System," in C. A. Keele, *The Assessment of Pain in Man and Animals* (Edinburgh: Livingstone, 1962).

[40] *Ibid.*, p. 131.

memory might never be stored. Once the memory is consolidated, however, neither the drug nor the jolt will have any effect. It takes several hours for the consolidation process to take place.[41]

In a host of experiments with animals, it was shown that neither sleep, nor drugs, nor shocks could erase memory. We may temporarily suppress the action of memory on behavior with the use of drugs, but we cannot make permanent changes. One implication of this is that in electroshock therapy, which is still used in a number of mental hospitals and clinics, there is a temporary loss of memory. Sometimes the memory loss lasts for a longer period of time and the person is made doubly anxious because he cannot remember. But shock treatment suppresses only the *consciousness* of the memory, not the memory itself. That memory still operates and produces anxiety. Clearly, Primal events and the neurosis based upon them are not easily dislodged from our systems. They are very much a part of our physiology. The only permanent way to erase the Primal events is to cut out part of our anatomy, as in lobotomy.

One of the implications of the time lag before memory is set down is that psychological hurts can be undone before they become permanent reverberating circuits. If a parent recognizes that he was tired and irritable when he snapped at his child for complaining, he can help his child feel that original feeling and the hurt of having it suppressed before it becomes locked away with Pain. It will then be just another memory, not a Primal one with enduring power. It will not be an added substratum for neurotic behavior. If the experience consolidates before it is completely felt, it will have to be relived later in order to be undone. This is not easily done when we try to recapture an event that happened twenty years in the past.

[41] This intricate process is discussed in detail by Roy John in his *Mechanisms of Memory* (New York: Academic Press, 1967).

7. THE FRONTAL CORTEX: THE NATURE OF CONSCIOUS AND UNCONSCIOUS FEELING

The Frontal Cortex

I have already noted the importance of the frontal lobe in the processing of reactions to pain. The frontal lobe acts on an integrated presentation of memory and its painful affect. Messages concerning feeling are interpreted in the frontal cortex and then relayed for activity to other areas. If the pain is too great, stimulation of the inhibitory activity of the hippocampus occurs. This results in limbic disconnection. Too much pain automatically activates the early survival mechanisms of repression, and the feeling gate is closed. However, the greater the pain, the greater is the frontal cortical activity to initiate repression.

What decisions the frontal areas make in regard to the incoming message will depend on what our history adds to it. A single rejection will be reacted to intensely because a history of rejection rides with it. Thus, when some of the nerve fibers of the prefrontal cortex are surgically severed from the thalamus, Primal history has been severed. The result is a calming effect because the person is reacting only to the present. The thalamic-temporal message no longer gets through. Pain has been surgically separated from its history and from its frontal processing plant. Memory and pain still exist, however; the *reaction* has been removed. Once the reaction is removed, the person will still know he is in pain but will have the attitude: "So what?" Lobotomies are still performed in mental hospitals today for those who are intractably tense and for those who suffer from chronic and severe organic pain, added evidence that tension is an undifferentiated form of pain.

What happens to people who have had Primal therapy is that they are freed from the *effects* of their Primal past. This occurs through connection to that past, as I have said. Being cut off from the connection to the past through a surgical disconnection confines the person to the present but also removes his only chance for final salvation and resolution. Lobotomy, in my opinion, severs the only hope for a person to regain his humanity. Again the dialectic: Connection to the past frees us from its effects; disconnection from the past keeps it there forever.

Once a person has had Primal Therapy, he still has his Primal memories, but they are shorn of the pain—hence of the power to provoke neurotic behavior. Feeling the pain means that the prefrontal cortex is no longer reading "terror" when feelings ascend. It is that terror—the terror of the consequences of the feeling—which elaborates a simple pain into total physiologic panic state. Experiencing the pain allows the feelings to be integrated and stored quietly. It is the frontal lobe which is ultimately responsible for a feeling's becoming painful. After a simple event, such as a teacher's criticism of a term paper, the temporal cortex scans the past for other criticisms and feeds all of the input to the frontal lobe for processing. One criticism would not be painful unless it had historic meaning—"My parents don't think I'm any good." It is the latent *meaning* in a single criticism which necessitates inhibition so that the organism is not flooded with pain. The *summation* of experience, then, not a single event, is what is crucial. Summation can occur and produce repression only when there is a Primal reservoir underneath.

We can see from the previous example of the homosexual that in neurotics meaning must be deflected (mother, and women, hurt) and a new meaning projected ("I can feel safe with men"). Thus bizarre and irrational ideas, mystical beliefs, and strange philosophies are all necessary buffers even in the most intelligent neurotics.

The Cortex as Defense

We are all aware of a time when someone leveled us with a criticism. From that point on we hear and see practically nothing. We believe that we are nervous, but what is happening is that all the resources of the body are engaged in the *old* primal battle. The frontal cortex is aroused by the reticular system to keep the old pain away. We can see this in electroencephalographic tracings of persons under stress. There is a large evoked potential which suggests that a significant part of the cortex has become activated to defend itself.

The fact that massed cortical action is a defense against pain suggests that it is one major factor in the actual development of man's cortex. We know from Krech's work that rats' brains actually grow in weight as a result of stimulation.[42] It is not so farfetched to think that one major factor in the development of man's cortex was growth as a result of stimulation by pain—or the danger of it.

There are several kinds of organic brain disorders, but one in particular is relevant to the current discussion. In a certain kind of aphasia, a person can express his feelings but he cannot explain them. He can say "Shit!" with feeling, but he could not tell you why he said it. He would have no idea why he was angry, for instance. This kind of aphasia is an indication that expressions of feeling are recorded on a level of the brain which is closer to the feeling centers. The ability to *explain* feelings would seem to be a more distant and higher function. One of the problems with psychoanalysis and other insight therapies is that those higher centers dealing with explanation are engaged, not the lower ones intimately associated with feeling. In other words, the conventional therapist deals with the defensive areas of the cortex and his patient becomes an inverted aphasic; he can explain his feelings but not feel them.

The problem of any insight therapy is that it does not produce those painful connections from the cotex to the lower brain centers. In order to produce the connection which is usually an infantile or early childhood set of experiences, the patient must be allowed to be that little child so that his early feelings are connected. An adult *explaining* feelings cannot produce the connections to the reverberating Primal circuits. The only unifying therapeutic experience, then, is reliving the early unresolved pains. No matter how correctly the cortex perceives the

[42] D. Krech *et al.*, "Modifying Brain Chemistry and Anatomy by Enrichment or Impoverishment of Experience," in G. Newton and S. Levine, *Early Experience and Behavior* (Springfield, Ill., 1968).

inner problem or the dynamics of the system's behavior, no matter how much insight exists, nothing can change without the connection.

This point is dramatically illustrated when patients relive a birth trauma. The unresolved pains of those experiences produce a lifelong tension in the same way that any Primal Pains do. No explanation in the world will undo that tension because its source has nothing to do with cerebral ideation. This is even truer when that explanation is offered by an expert—a therapist. Each person has his own historic truth. He can be overeating because his mother was always angry, because his father was cold, because his sister was mean, and for all of those reasons. Those reasons can become apparent to him only when the feelings arise which indicate by their force both the source of the underlying motivation and their strength.

Even if an explanation of a patient's behavior were perfect, the underlying Primal circuits would still be activating the system, safely insulated from the explanation. Because explanation and the feelings are two distinct entities (unless of course the explanation arises *as a result* of a Primal feeling experience), there is no way for explanation to change anything. Primal circuits are not explained away.

Cerebral ideation, even when it is called an "insight," rides above the split, which is why no book on psychology can help a neurotic "get straight." He can know all and feel nothing. One can change one's conscious values and goals so that the energy which previously drove one to be a compulsive thief can now drive him to "constructive" overwork, but the sickness, the Pain, remains.

8. DISCONNECTION, GENERALIZATION, AND PSYCHOSIS

Gantt has noted that the organism continuously responds to old emotional memories, preparing itself for "acts no longer required." [43] Thus, he notes, instead of a

[43] W. H. Gantt, "Principles of Nervous Breakdown," *Annals of the New York Academy of Science*, Vol. 56, No. 143 (1953).

specific reaction—a clenched fist—there is a general one —elevated blood pressure. Once a feeling is repressed and no longer specific (because a specific feeling means pain), it generalizes. Smythies states, "It is possible that the elaboration of reactions to stress, anxiety and depression is conducted by these circuits [limbic] which would be responsible for setting thresholds and degree of generalization of these emotional reactions." [44] In other words, initial pain does not become an elaborated reaction. Instead of a specific fear ("I am unloved and therefore alone"), there is amorphous discomfort and agitation. The fear may generalize to other neutral situations which are not intrinsically fearful. Thus we see that a neurotic reaction is one not appropriate to the situation, such as inordinate fear of crowds.

The cortex, not directly connected to the structures processing the sensation of the original feeling, cannot help in the process of discriminating its quality and source, and as a result there is generalization. A fear of father early in life, inhibited, becomes first a vague, fearful feeling around father, then of men and authorities, and then a generalized fearful state. The fear is real, though not specific. It remains as vague anxiety focused at random in the present, focused on those things in the present which are symbolic of the feeling, such as fear of policemen as father surrogates. The fear may become a phobia when the source is thought to be of heights, or it may develop into paranoia where the source is believed to be enemy aliens. Paranoia is an extension of the fear, generalized more broadly because the fear is so great the threshold of response is lowered and almost anything can set the fear going. To block the feeling, the cortex is mobilized to construct a completely unreal world to ensure that nothing can penetrate. What happens, then, is that fear becomes a viable entity operating in the diencephalon and reticular systems, while the cortex can only approximate the real fear. The symbolic cortical content is a product of the real feeling in the same way that dream symbols are referents or associations from repressed feelings. The basis of the fear of enemy aliens may be: "I'm all alone and alienated from everyone." The catastrophic all-alone, alienated feeling is then blocked and rechanneled cortically into "the aliens." In a dialectic swing, inventing aliens who are watching is the way some psychotics keep from feeling alone and alienated.

The sequence of the split or disconnection begins with a sensory input—a sight, smell, or sound which is perceived as something dangerous (an angry look by one's mother will do). This perception is interpreted by the cortex as dangerous; the reticular system galvanizes the body for danger and relays its message either through the thalamus or directly back to the cortex, where cortical tissue is engaged in order to inhibit the feeling evoked by the original perception. In plain language, mother's angry look means: "I'm bad. She won't take care of me"; the exact feeling is severed, and the system, now tense, is galvanized toward pleasing mother instead of feeling the total rejection. Instead of being afraid of his mother's rejection, the child is afraid of the dark or of spiders or of school. The disconnected feeling is generalized to symbols. Dealing with the symbolic behavior, discussing the fear of school, for example, will do nothing to resolve the neurosis. To delve into all the symbolic actions is to get lost in a maze of symbols which are only *derivatives* of the feeling. The symbolic actions are endless and very complex, but the basic source of the neurosis is not.

The greater the cortical spread of the old feeling in one's current life, the more neurotic or psychotic the person. A man who complains that his wife is trying to undermine him might be thought of as neurotic and simply given counseling. A man who stretches this notion to a belief that every girl in his office building is trying to undermine him might well be considered insane. Enormous pain has expanded his symbolization over more and more aspects of his life until quantity passes into quality and neurosis shifts into psychosis. It is this expansion quality that often makes a psychotic delusion seem so bizarre—it is completely at odds with reality. The actual cortical area involved in generalization of nervous activity is increased. Thus, the psychotic is unable to deal with reality and care for himself, since his cortex is diffusely and completely engaged with the past.

Psychosis means that the cortex is increasingly involved in the underlying feelings. The person becomes lost in his symbols because they *are* his feelings transmuted. When the connections of the orbito-frontal cortex are severed from the thalamus, it follows that there is less generalized, symbolic behavior. This is because the driving Primal feeling is no longer pushing the cortex to act. We need not resort to surgery, however, since tranquilizers can produce a similar effect.

To reconnect correctly is to dispel symbolic acts, and undo neurosis, irrespective of its form. Until that reconnection, aspects of consciousness disengaged from their *feeling* counterpart become two viable entities waging an unconscious war with each other for the rest of the person's life. The reason there have been so many approaches to neurosis is that therapists have been dealing with cortical flight instead of the dynamics of disconnection.

9. THE PROCESS OF CURE

The purpose of a neurophysiologic model of mental illness is to lay the groundwork for the reversal of such an illness. I have noted that any cure of mental illness must involve access to the Primal circuits. Let us see how this happens in Primal Therapy.

In ordinary life, the neurotic is upset about something —say, a criticism by a superior—and his neurotic behavior is set in motion. He may placate the superior, deny the event, and get a headache or become furious and lose his temper or simply pout all day. He may also project blame onto someone else. He is, in short, working off the charge of the triggered Primal circuit—something which may mean: "We don't love you." In Primal Therapy, we trigger that same circuit by numerous means so that it is activated. We may do this in a very simple way by having the patient discuss the criticism by the superior and re-direct the discussion to criticism by his parents. The techniques for reactivating key circuits are quite complex and beyond the purview of this discussion. Once the circuits are activated, the usual ploy of the patient is automatically to defend in his characteristic way. Shallow breathing may be one small aspect of a defense. The patient may also stiffen up, tighten his abdominal muscles, and begin a verbal barrage of excuses. In Primal Therapy each avenue of defense, both physiologic and psychologic, is blocked (again by techniques complex and varied) so that the feeling becomes stronger and closer to consciousness. Making the patient shake his body loosely and wildly at precisely the right moment may help break the physical armor. At the same time, recognizing the totality of any single defense, many other techniques are employed to render the patient defenseless—feelingful.

At a certain critical level the Primal feelings can no longer be held back, and they overtake the patient. He is truly defenseless against them as they rise to put him in great agony and then release. The agony is a result of the press of a feeling—"They don't like me"—which has clustered around it many thousands of memory events, each adding its bit of pain. It is easy to understand why such blocked pain can produce catastrophic illness and distort the body physically, and why the release into consciousness of those painful circuits can produce such violent reactions. Hallucinogenic drugs release those circuits in random fashion and may release too much, resulting in *more* symbolic ideation, rather than less.

What is important to understand is that it is not the scream, the thrashing about, the pounding of the pillows, which is critical. It is the *connection* which finally and ultimately releases the person from his tension in a permanent way. Screaming and pounding in and of themselves offer only temporary surcease.

Let us look at one example to clarify this. In group therapy one day I criticized a psychologist-patient for acting stupidly. He began a host of verbal defenses, using big words, scientific language, and elegant rationales. I stopped him from saying anything while beleaguering him with valid criticisms. He already had a number of Primals previously and so was relatively defenseless. He fell over onto the floor and began salivating. In a few minutes, one could hear infantile wails which became louder and louder and lasted some thirty minutes. What had happened? Very early in life, as soon as he could think and reason, he began to "figure out" what he could do to survive with extremely harsh and rejecting parents. He used his "brain" to defend himself. This continued throughout school. He became a psychologist, still "figuring out" problems—or figuring his way out of problems. In group therapy that day, I stopped his verbalizations and "thinking." Because he was already vulnerable to pain, because he had already connected and released a number of pains previously which opened him up toward tolerating more, he was thrown into the time *before* he could figure out and defend against rejection—when all he could do was wail. My rejection that day tiggered an old circuit.

What the psychologist-patient was really defending against that day in the group was not me but that early, catastrophic rejection. Any confrontation with me, any "working it through" in group, any screaming at me or at group members, would avail nothing. The aims were those early memories.

To reawaken a patient's past we will do anything from bringing a live puppy into therapy to supplying stuffed teddy bears and playpens. These are meaningless to defended (repressed) persons, but highly charged for those more vulnerable. These are used, however, only as activating mechanisms and not as ends in themselves.

After a Primal experience insights abound; the person, now properly connected, becomes immediately flooded with all of his misdirected and rechanneled efforts—wanting his wife to be his mother, for example. The continuous misdirected behavior in the neurotic is what causes him to live his life in fragments, each event being a thing-unto-itself. To put it all together means pain, so he lives his life compartmentalized. Primal feelings tie those disparities together. Feeling one's helplessness helps a patient understand his dependence on teachers, children, doctors, and so on. Feeling the hate toward his mother helps him understand his relationships to *all* women. Without the feeling base, each contact with a woman, for example, produces hostility, carefully rationalized and justified. In short, when his life is cut off from its historic base, he is left to flounder without perspective.

The key to cure is the systematic opening of the hippocampal gate. Each connection means less of a load on this structure. Each felt Pain indicates one less weight to keep the "gate" closed and one more step toward producing a totally feeling human being. A more fluid gate means a more integrated and connected person whose feelings will not be blocked and diverted into neurotic channels. The ultimate aim of psychotherapy must be to unblock this structure and release its storehouse of Pain-laden memories. I submit that nearly all forms of therapy extant circumvent this structure and merely redivert the already diverted feeling into other more socially acceptable channels.

There are many ways to gain access to this storehouse. Massage can do it if key muscle systems are used to bind tension. Hypnosis can help by temporarily lulling conscious controls. Drugs, such as sodium amytal, certainly can accomplish it by producing the same effect. But I believe that these techniques are random and do not accomplish what is the essence of Primal Therapy—a *systematic* carefully titrated release of Pain.

The "cure" or final point of health occurs when each old painful feeling is linked to its precise origins. The person is left with no generalized drives from the past, and thus no neurosis.

10. CONCLUSIONS

In conclusion, feelings are the essential nature of man. They are neither good nor bad, constructive nor destructive. They are. Being natural is what is intrinsic to all forms of life. Neurosis is a result of a disruption in the smooth integration of higher and lower brain functions. To block any natural process is to set in motion a force toward unification. That force in neurotics takes the form of tension. We need to be whole. Neurosis keeps us going by dividing us from those painful feelings which threaten the integrity of the system. But at the same time it produces the dynamism for integration.

Our systems are repositories of the truth. The brain (and the body) preserves what is real no matter how devious and entwined our cortical thought processes become. A lie of the mind means a hurt of the body. Conversely, too much hurt *produces* lies in the mind. The system retains our truths because they happened to us. They are part of our experience whether we acknowledge them consciously or not. We finally break down from those unacknowledged truths. Only man is capable of conceptualizing his sensations into feelings; only he can put it all together, yet he seldom does.

The neurotic must eventually break down. Because of the constant activation of his system, the weakest and most susceptible part of his body will be affected first. A predisposition to allergies will ultimately end in a full-blown allergy of one kind or another. Symptomatic relief is always possible, but until one resolves the lower brain activation, more symptoms will occur. Sickness demands its symptoms.

Once the body's functions become distorted, we must take care not to study them apart from the total system; this error can lead to only partial truths—the kind of partial truths found in ahistoric psychologic theories which deal predominantly with symptoms and not generating causes. There is evidence, for example, of faulty potassium metabolism in some schizophrenics; to conclude from this dysfunction that faulty metabolism is a *cause* of schizophrenia would be unwarranted. It is more likely that most of us are born quite healthy and become distorted and sick because of Primal stress. This is apparent in post-Primal patients who return to good health once the inside stressors are removed. The fact that we often see soft-tissue growth in these individuals must be related to a return to proper endocrine function. Unfortunately, in some patients physical dysfunctions have persisted for so many years that irreparable damage occurs and nothing can alter that state.

What is clear is that suppression of self is not simply a matter of psychological processes. It is the suppression of aspects of one's whole biologic system—the biologic system which mediates our feelings. I believe that many neurotics have not grown to their full genetic potential because of this suppression.[45]

What I am emphasizing is that *all* disease must be seen in relation to feelings, for feelings predominate and integrate human functioning. *Not feeling* disintegrates human functioning. Feelings are to be felt or man is not human. "Even the most discordant events are directed by feelings aroused by them. The emotion always urges to penetrate everything that goes on in us, to quench resistance, or rechannel it, and to impose its own total rhythm throughout our inner life." [46] This was written in 1928.

Not only is the cortex powerless to stop lower brain center activation, but the fact of cortical isolation from feeling centers means that neurotics are compelled to act impulsively and irrationally owing to the pressure from this activation. It means that the neurotic cannot help himself (as in the need for drugs) and, most importantly, cannot change in any profound way. He can give up his symptoms only for a time. Primal pressure not only distorts one's physical system, then, but makes the neurotic act out in the world even against his will—smoking is a good example. He must relieve that pressure somehow. Not being able to connect himself, he must do the next best thing. He must do what most doctors do—treat himself symptomatically. Smoking is the "pill" he uses to ease his tension.

The more pain, the more likely he is to act out. If his home environment completely straitjacketed him from acting out, then the full weight of the pressure will cause the inner organs to give way that much faster—heart attacks, ulcers, diabetes, and so on.

The pressure on the mind causes the same flight reaction, only we call it the manic flight of ideas. The person's

[45] See Hans Selye, "Stress and Disease," in C. B. Reed, I. E. Alexander, and S. Tomkins, *Psychopathology* (Cambridge, Mass.: Harvard University Press, 1963).

[46] F. Krueger, "Das Wesen der Gefuhle," *Archives f.d. Ges. Psychol.*, Vol. 65 (1928), pp. 91–123.

mind becomes a pool of distractions; he cannot concentrate or listen because the pressure is driving him on. Connection ends all the pressure, physically and mentally.

What is the unconscious? It is merely inhibited consciousness, those buried needs and feelings which drive the neurotic and shape his experience each minute of his life. Primal events in the brain are like a series of freeways, looping and turning but going nowhere because the areas of the brain that could be interpreting them are involved in deflecting their meaning and misinterpreting them. It is involved, in short, in saving the person from great pain—which is what connection to proper meaning produces. Penfield indicates this tangentially when he says: "This functional unit [the interpretive cortex] is partially separable from the overall activity of the brain."[47]

What I have said here necessarily has been oversimplified. The research on the consolidation of memory constitutes volumes already. There are more structures involved in the processing of pain than I have noted.[48] For example, we react physically to pain. It shows in our faces, our posture, and our arm movements. The structure involved with refining these movements is the cerebellum. Two investigators have found that when this structure is destroyed, the *experience* of pain is markedly reduced. Reaction, therefore, constitutes part of the *total* pain experience. One wonders if the fact that many children are not allowed to even react to their hurts, does not in itself inure them to feeling. If you can't do anything about pain, the only thing left is to repress it.[49]

What should be clear by now is that one cannot cure the mind and the body separately. There can be no liberating intellectual experiences or any exercises or messages which can free the body. Massages of muscle groups are

[47] Penfield and Perot, *op. cit.*, p. 692.
[48] R. Melzak and P. D. Wall, "Sensory Processes and Perception," in *Brain and Behavior*, ed. by K. Pribram, Vol. 2 (Baltimore: Penguin, 1969), pp. 145–157.
[49] See also Magda Arnold, *Nature of Emotions* (Baltimore: Penguin, 1968), p. 321, for discussion of cerebellar destruction and its effects. Experiments on the cerebellum quoted herein were carried out by Sprague and Chambers.

as random as free association; neither is related to specific causes of tension in the brain, therefore neither can do anything permanent. Letting the mind run chaotically is not freedom. "Blowing one's mind" with drugs is not freedom, nor is floating the body in a warm pool. Freedom for neurotics is brought about only by connecting to what is constricting them, to those memories which produce tension. Once there is connection the mind can really be free to do something besides run from pain—and the muscles will stop their running as well.

The Primal position is essentially Darwinian: The development of man's higher brain is partly a result of his need to cope with danger. One of the central dangers in his evolution was the organization of society itself. Man's cortex may have had to grow just because in organized society he could not act on his feelings as he willed. He had to inhibit himself and become submerged to the dictates of the social structure. In order to inhibit, he needed more cortex. It was the cortex which made feelings opprobrious. It was the cortex which perverted and blocked feelings when they became inimical to society's needs. Feelings became bad or good in relation to how they suited society's requirements. Feelings became dangerous. As society grew, feelings became trampled under concepts such as "respect," "reverence," "loyalty," and "obedience." Thus were the seeds of neurosis sown. It was the cortical concepts, not the so-called animalistic instincts, which set man against other men. It was when men would not be loyal or reverent that they were punished. What is beautiful is natural, and what is ugly is nature deformed. The deforming of natural man is the beginning of human destruction.

Closing down against pain is a factor in nearly all organic life. The ability to close down consciousness is only an extension of a process of withdrawal from irritation that began with the single-celled amoeba. Consciousness is no more than an aggregation of cells functioning in a complex way. It is but another function of organic tissue, part of the constriction process ranging from the narrowing of blood vessels with pain to the constriction of the pupils when the input is too severe either physically (sunlight) or psychologically. *Neurosis, then, is a normal physiologic response to pain.* Its processes can be understood in the same way that other constrictive processes can—response to pain and threat. To understand what drives neurosis is to lay bare the fundamental structure of neurosis.

Neurosis occurs because experiences not necessarily catastrophic in and of themselves summate at some point early in the child's life and become the adequate stimulus to cause a narrowing of consciousness. The summation point I call the major Primal Scene. It is traumatic because it is summative, the consolidation of a host of previous minor insults.

As time goes on and we learn more about memory storage, particularly the storage of painful memories, it is not inconceivable that neurosis can be altered by electronic probes which set off pains in ordered sequence. Certainly, this is precisely what Primals do. Psychologically induced Primals ultimately become electrically induced events in the nervous system. Perhaps, someday, there will be a way to circumvent the psychological stimulus and go straight to the areas of the brain which require triggering. There are drugs today such as LSD which release a flood of old feelings and memories; they are released in random fashion, but who knows whether drugs cannot someday be much more specific.

In final summary: Painful and unacceptable messages are organized below the level of conscious awareness; the body reacts to pain of which it is unaware, and this pain sets in motion a lifetime of behaviors involving flight, both mentally and physically. There is only one way neurosis can be undone—to relive and resolve those early, unconscious Primal Pains. The fact that Primal Theory can be integrated with neuropsychology is the fundamental reason for its predictive and therapeutic quality.

BIBLIOGRAPHY

Chapman and Knowles. "Effect of Phenothiazines on Disordered Thought in Schizophrenics," *Journal of Consultative Psychology*, 28:165 (1964).

Gellhorn, Ernest. *Autonomic-Somatic Integrations*. Minneapolis: University of Minnesota Press, 1967.

————. *Biological Foundations of Emotion*. Chicago: Scott, Foresman, Co., 1968.

Hilgard, Ernest R. *The Experience of Hypnosis*. New York: Harcourt, Brace and World, 1965.

John, E. Roy. *Mechanisms of Memory*. New York: Academic Press, 1967.

Lawson, Chester A. *Brain Mechanism and Human Learning*. Boston: Houghton Mifflin, 1967.

Lesse, Stanley. *An Evaluation of the Results of the Psychotherapic*. Springfield, Ill.: Charles Thomas Co., 1968.

Mandell, A. J., and Mandell, M. P. *Psychochemical Research in Man*. New York: Academic Press, 1969.

Reed, C. F., Alexander, I. E., and Tomkins, Silvan. *Psychopathology*. Cambridge, Mass.: Harvard University Press, 1963.

Soretsky, Theodore. "Effects of Chlorpromazine on Primary Process Thought Manifestations," *Journal of Abnormal and Social Psychology*, 71:247 (Aug., 1966).

Widen, L. *Recent Advances in Clinical Neurophysiology*. New York: Elseview Pub. Co., 1967.

APPENDIX

The following diagrams indicate how a feeling may be blocked and rechanneled both downward into the body and upward to areas of the cerebral cortex to produce symbolic ideation. The key system involved in the blocking is the limbic system, which is a harmonious interconnection of brain structures concerned with the storage, regulation, and control of feeling. Blocked feelings reverberate within the limbic system as "trapped" memory circuits. (Illustrations conceived by Lee Woldenberg, M.D., and executed by Jill Penkhus.)

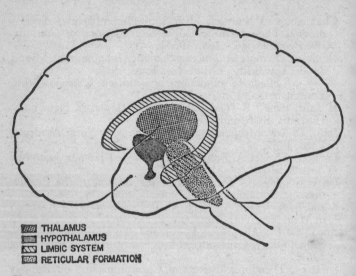

▨ THALAMUS
▨ HYPOTHALAMUS
▨ LIMBIC SYSTEM
▨ RETICULAR FORMATION

FIGURE I

This cross section shows the brainstem and cortex: The reticular system extends through the brainstem. Shown also are the hypothalamus, thalamus, and hippocampus of the limbic system. The hippocampus underlies the limbic cortex of the temporal lobe.

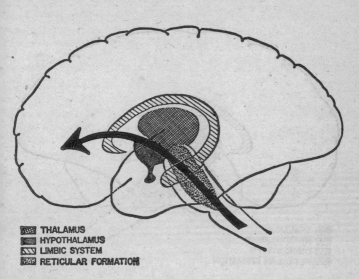

THALAMUS
HYPOTHALAMUS
LIMBIC SYSTEM
RETICULAR FORMATION

FIGURE 2

Sensory input from all sensory organs stimulates the reticular activating system in the reticular formation to alert the frontal cortex. This activation is nonspecific.

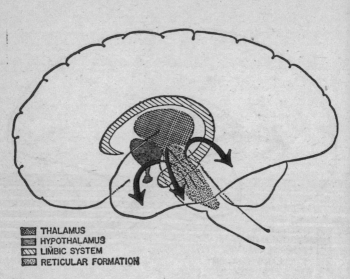

THALAMUS
HYPOTHALAMUS
LIMBIC SYSTEM
RETICULAR FORMATION

FIGURE 3

As in Figure 2, the temporal cortex is activated by the reticular activating system. The entire brain is alerted to receive information.

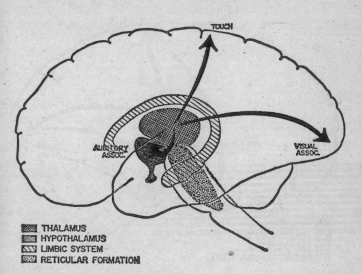

FIGURE 4

The stimulus, perhaps a parental reprimand, is really a combination of separate stimuli (sight, sound, touch, smell), and all are relayed by the thalamus to their appropriate receiving areas in the cortex. For example, the auditory stimulus of the reprimand, an angry sound, passes from the auditory receiving area to an area where the sounds acquire association with the words used. As the impulse passes through cortical tissue, meaning is acquired. These latter areas are termed association areas.

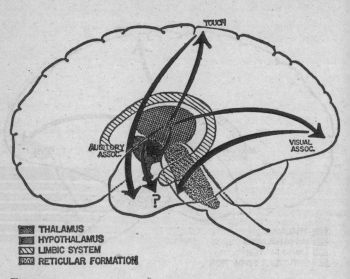

THALAMUS
HYPOTHALAMUS
LIMBIC SYSTEM
RETICULAR FORMATION

FIGURE 5

As the stimuli in each receiving area travel through the specific association areas, they acquire meaning for that particular event. If any
parts of the stimulus are similar to old (painful) scenes, this information
appears to be combined somewhere in the temporal regions of the limbic
lobe. The scene is no longer experienced "in the present." Old pains
joined to the present scene have been activated. They are then projected
together to the frontal cortex for interpretation.

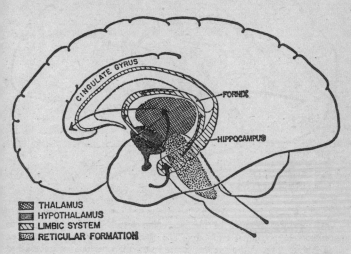

FIGURE 6

In this simplified drawing, the combined stimulus from Figure 5 achieves conscious awareness in the following manner: It passes from the limbic cortex of the temporal lobe into the hippocampus, through another limbic structure called the fornix to the posterior part of the hypothalamus. Finally, it is continued to the thalamus for relay to the cingulate gyrus (cortical tissue underlying the frontal cortex). The conscious awareness of the stimulus and its full meaning ("They do not love me") is felt.

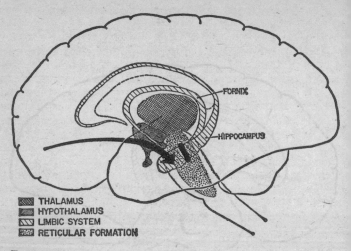

FORNIX

HIPPOCAMPUS

THALAMUS
HYPOTHALAMUS
LIMBIC SYSTEM
RETICULAR FORMATION

FIGURE 7

The painful meaning of the reprimand forces the frontal cortex to stimulate hippocampal inhibition. The block results from this signal of the frontal lobe. Although the transmission to conscious awareness has been stopped, the aroused feelings have access to lower brain centers which innervate the whole body. The body reacts to the meaning of the stimulus even though there is no conscious awareness (blood pressure increases, muscles contract, sweating occurs, etc.). The system is reacting to its unresolved history. Because of blocking in the hippocampus, the painful feeling of being unloved is also rechanneled to other brain centers which rationalize, project, and otherwise misinterpret the feeling. These rechanneled impulses are the misdirected, neurotic connections which occur because the direct connection has been blocked owing to the painful impact of the stimulus and its related history.

II. Sleep, Dreams, and Mental Illness

Let us now discuss the relationship of dreams to mental illness; or, since symbolic dreams *are* mental illness, I shall point out why this is so, drawing on current sleep and dream research wherever indicated. The central source of reference will be *The Biology of Dreaming*, by E. Hartmann,[1] a compendium of many hundreds of separate research studies which represents, in my opinion, the latest and most comprehensive body of work on the subject. Hartmann's work contains several quotes: the eminent neurophysiologist Hughlings Jackson wrote, "Find out about dreams and you will find out about insanity"—a most prophetic statement, paraphrased by Carl Jung, who said, "Let the dreamer walk about and act like one awakened and we have the clinical picture of dementia praecox." A great deal of research has shown the truth of these statements, written decades ago.

I have already discussed reverberating circuits which reside as memory units in the brain, producing neural and systemic effects. These are continuous innervations which remain for a lifetime, both day and night, whether one is awake or asleep. The energy of the memory circuit is continually rechanneled to symbolic or associative areas of the brain instead of making the straight connection to Pain. Those rechanneled impulses become hallucinations, bizarre ideas, or dreams and nightmares. In other words, the dream is the symbolic derivative of the Primal memory circuit. It is a phenomenon not different from awake ideation; both are symbolic of feelings. When the feelings connect, ideation is direct and straight; and we would expect this to show up both in straight ideas during the day and nonsymbolic mental processes while asleep.

The mind and the body each has its own way of showing the sickness. Crazy ideas—"They always laugh behind my back"—are the mental manifestations of a *systemic* illness. Bizarre dreams are the mental abberations in our

[1] E. Hartmann, *The Biology of Dreaming* (Springfield, Ill.: Charles Thomas, 1967).

sleep. Bleeding ulcers are the "craziness" of the body. The misdirected neural impulses exert pressure on the mind and the body. We don't have straight ideas during the day and get sick in the mind during sleep. We *hide* our crazy ideas better during the day, keep them to ourselves, and "maintain"; during sleep, with our consciousness less vigilant, the true sickness is apparent. That is why understanding symbolic dreams is such an accurate index of mental illness.

Brain structures and brain interrelationships do not change just because we are not awake. Grooved misconnections which have existed for decades in the brain remain stable and direct the forms of dreams. The fact that both the body and the mind absorb and release Primal pressure means that one can use either to relieve tension. Thus, one can work himself into exhaustion or dance all night or have intense sex and release enough tension to provide restful sleep. The next night, however, without the bodily release, the tension returns and may produce sleeplessness or nightmares. The person may wake out of that nightmare feeling exceptionally tense; but the nightmare did not produce the tension—tension produced the nightmare.

So the first point to be made about symbolic dreams is that they are not disparate events, isolated from waking behavior. They are different aspects of the identical neurological processes. Defenses are automatic and unconscious, as shown by the fact that we remain defended and symbolic in our sleep.

When someone awakens out of a nightmare we see how automatic our defenses are—we become conscious to keep from being conscious of our feelings. We use consciousness to remain unconscious of Pain. When things are too unpleasant socially, if our children have glaring faults we dare not acknowledge, or if a friend is suddenly hostile, we may inhibit consciousness, become unconscious of the fact.

We can be both neurotic and psychotic in our sleep. Instead of acting out the craziness, our dream characters do it for us. How bizarre the dream depends on the amount of underlying Pain which drives the mind increasingly away from the feeling. Dreams then become a natural index of the degree of mental illness. The more complex and bizarre they are, the deeper the sickness. They are reliable indicators because they cannot be faked, nor can they be changed by an act of will, as we might attempt with our waking behavior.

Dreams and nightmares are not persistent events. They ebb and flow; they are rhythmic. We are mentally ill in cycles. Or, rather we *show* our illness in cycles.

The cycle of the *manifestations* of mental illness (dreams, hallucinations) is as predictable as the cycle of body temperature. Repression of the underlying Primal circuits is not static; repression ebbs and flows. Repression changes for two reasons. First, outside triggering events can make the underlying circuit more active. Second, anything that causes a weakening of defenses, such as sleep, lessens cortical repression and thereby permits ascent of feelings (and the need to symbolize). Ordinarily, repression does its job automatically (circuits are blocked and rerouted through a complicated neurochemical process as outlined in the section on neurophysiology) so that one does not feel tense or anxious and Primal circuits lie dormant owing to the effectiveness of repression.

Human life seems to be a series of continuing cycles, ranging from the changing of the tides to the daily changes in temperature and the monthly estrous cycle. Man's evolution has been inextricably bound with cycle changes in his environment, and his inner environment has become an extension of that cyclic movement.

The evidence in dream research indicates that we release tension in measurable cycles. What seems to happen is that when neurotic man becomes overloaded with Pain (tension), he must begin sloughing off his tension both night and day. The sloughing-off cycle *is* neurotic behavior. At night it takes the form of symbolic dreams— feelings that begin to ascend into consciousness activate the cortex to produce a story to explain the activation. The story is subconscious—a dream. The story we produce during the day against that very same activation can be called an irrational thought. It need not be any more rational than the dream. Both the symbolic dream and irrational thoughts are tension-releasing mechanisms. They are the mental spillways of the cyclic sloughing-off process. To block these mental manifestations is to produce either a Primal or, more likely, more severe mental illness. That is why one cannot be readily argued out of a hallucination (or theory), any more than one could be argued out of his dreams. When the hallucination is blocked, say, through the use of drugs, what is likely to result is more severe nightmares—sleep psychosis. If one were to block all neurotic outlets (smoking, drinking, sex, etc.), we might again find a more "strained" dream life in the form of psychotic dreams. It would not be a different disease; it would be a different aspect of the same disease—the buildup of Pain.

As we shall see in a moment, the release cycle is mediated by a chemical known as serotonin. Before exploring the direct evidence, it might be well to take a brief look at man's history of sleep. Most humans need about eight hours of sleep on the average. The ability to sleep peacefully is necessary to conserve energy; our metabolic rate (the amount of energy burned) drops during sleep. In this respect, sleep, especially restful sleep, is one important way we prolong our lives. Even though sleep is necessary for survival, there was a time in man's early history when it was extremely dangerous for him to be unconscious for too long a period of time. In some kind of evolutionary compromise, primitive man slept in cycles, possibly rising to consciousness every hour and a half to check his surroundings and then dropping back to sleep once again. As man progressed and as external dangers receded, it was no longer necessary for survival to wake up periodically and check out the environment; soon we only approximated that state—we rose to *near-consciousness* every so often. This near-conscious state was a defensive evolutionary legacy. This ninety-minute near-conscious state (in terms of electroencephalographic readings) is variously known as "dream-state," "paradoxical sleep" (because it resembles waking), REM (rapid eye movement) sleep, and, as Hartmann terms it, "D-state." He calls it "D-state" because he believes this state has properties other than just dreaming.

The D-state occurs every ninety minutes during an eight-hour sleep cycle, lasting about twenty minutes. These states occur just after our deepest stage of sleep, which makes sound evolutionary sense in terms of ready-ing us for an integrated defense against danger after be-ing completely and deeply unconscious. The danger in modern man is not from predatory animals, but from his Primal feelings.

The D-state is characterized by an elevated brain tem-perature indicative of the increased brain activity. Asso-ciated with elevated brain temperature is an elevated blood pressure, more rapid pulse, higher respiration rate, changes in pupil size and in muscle movements, and a slightly elevated body temperature. All of this is coinci-dent with a more complete flaccidity of the musculature. It is a time when the brain is galvanized to defend the body. If we remember that Primal pressure is contained both mentally and physically via a rigid and tight mus-culature, then when that musculature relaxes, the mind is forced to exert a greater defense. In neurologic terms, the forebrain becomes more tonically active at a time when the physical system is relatively defenseless. This is the time that dreams occur.

The mind—the thinking, imagining cortex—is not en-gaged in a continuous, steady activity; it must rest just as the body must rest. Perhaps the term dream-state cycle is a misnomer, for there is evidence for a ninety-minute cycle during waking, as well. Hartmann discusses a study of one person who went without sleep for two hundred hours. He "experienced episodes of hallucinations and disoriented behavior approximately every ninety minutes, perhaps at the times when he would have been dreaming if allowed to sleep" (1962). Perhaps the waking cycle occurs in lesser form, making its detection difficult, or perhaps we humans are engaged in so much activity dur-ing the day that the cycle is masked and unrecognized.

We do see evidence of the ninety-minute cycle during waking in phenomena such as alcoholic withdrawal. There is evidence by Greenberg (1966) and Gross *et al.* (1965) that delirium tremens occur every ninety minutes and represent the "breakthrough" of the D mechanism into waking life—the waking dream. Research at Montefiore Hospital in New York found that migraine headaches which occur at night begin during D-states. They noted that daytime attacks may be due to a state similar to the dream state.

Sexual perversions can be seen as another aspect of the waking dream. An ascending Primal feeling of "Momma, I feel like a girl" may force a man to run out and exhibit himself to quell that feeling in the same way we produce a dream ritual to mask it. (We would need to clock these impulses to see if they manifested any periodicity.) The perverted ritual relieves tension in the same way as the dream; the pervert can stop his acting out when the dream is no longer necessary—that is, when the tension overload is diminished. Acting out for perverts is every bit as important in maintaining psychic economy as symbolic dreams. We jail those who cannot contain the ritual within the sleep cycle.

The implication of all this is that there is a continuous alert-release cycle in all of us. It is generally agreed that the ninety-minute release periods are essential to proper functioning. Deprivation of these states produces what I call "Primal Rebound." Primal Rebound results from the accumulation of tension which occurs when neurotic outlets are blocked. Tranquilizing drugs can mask Primal Pain, preventing the sloughing-off process from occurring; the accumulated pressure will move against the mental-physical system, producing either more bizarre dreams or sequelae such as coronary attacks (there is evidence that angina attacks occur more frequently in dream states).

Generally, drugs suppress Pains for ten to twenty hours, but when drugs are suddenly removed, Pains ascend with redoubled force, requiring the person to take more tranquilizers or sleeping pills. Accumulated Pain requires even more suppression, hence the need for (and tolerance to) stronger doses. We can readily see how someone becomes dependent on sleeping pills and tranquilizers: they are required to quell the same Pain, day and night.

One tranquilizer, for example, inhibits hallucinations and delusions, blocks D-states (also known as Rapid Eye

Movement, or REM sleep), and quiets us down so that we can sleep. The drug is known as a specific antitension, antianxiety agent, but the fact that its central effect is to diminish the *experience* (conscious awareness) of Pain should indicate that tension is unconnected, unconscious Pain. We usually don't feel the Pain; we experience what it does to us—makes us feel edgy and agitated, speeds up the mind, and keeps us awake.

If pain-killers diminish D-states, there must be some connection between dreaming and Pain. Those with less Pain should have less symbolic dreams and perhaps a shortened D-state period.[2] (Current research in our laboratory clarifies and confirms these points.*) What is clear now is that reduced Primal Pain reduces the symbolism of dreams: less Pain, less neurosis.

The fact that a single pain-killing drug can affect such seemingly diverse behaviors as hallucinations and symbolic dreams indicates that they both may result from the same underlying process. The more one stays tranquilized while awake, the greater the rebound potential and the heavier the dose of sleeping pills required to maintain restful sleep. The dose required is commensurate with the amount of Pain. For example, before therapy one patient took sixty Placidil in a serious suicide attempt. Though he was unconscious for almost four days, he did not die. His life was saved, I believe, by the inordinate amount of Pain which kept his brain activated even under a lethal dose of tranquilizers. After therapy, it would probably have taken fewer pills to put him away permanently. We can see the effect of the rebound in the withdrawal symptoms of drug addicts; the body convulses from the sudden onrush of so much Pain. The sudden assault by accumulated Pain in addiction withdrawal is very much

* The assumption is that REM sleep is related to Pain. Our research should help clarify this problem. Preliminary indications already corroborate this point. If patients with less Pain have less REM sleep, the hypothesis would be verified. This means post-Primal patients have more restful and relaxed sleep with less overall dream life.
* See "Research," Part V.

like what happens to a sleeping person who has been heavily tranquilized during the day. He sweats, shakes, screams out in pain, but calls it a nightmare.

Serotonin is a key chemical agent which facilitates inhibition of nerve impulses and thus aids in repression. All of us manufacture it. An overload of Pain tends to "use up" the supply. A study at Stanford University, for example, found that depressives have low serotonin values.

Here is what Torda says about serotonin: "By blocking the transmission of reticular activating system impulses to the hippocampal pyramidal cells, serotonin release decreases hippocampal theta activity generation." [3] There is an increase in cerebral activation with a relative decrease of the hippocampal inhibitory (theta) activity. That is, as inhibition of lower impulses is weakened, there is increased cortical action as a sort of compensation. In Primal terms, as Primal memories have egress to higher centers, these higher centers must go into action and produce dreams to cover or symbolize them. Torda puts it this way: "Dreams (as visual concomitants of processes involved in the consolidation of long-term memory) *enter awareness through decrease of pertinent inhibitory processes* [my emphasis] serving to prevent perception of these consolidation processes." [4] In short, the hippocampus serves to block awareness of memory.

In sleep, when there is a slowing of the hippocampal theta, dream life begins. The person who can remember his dreams is no doubt less repressed than the one who cannot, for the latter kind of person seems to have inhibited even the symbolic derivatives of the underlying Pain. I think that this is a function of great Primal Pain where total blockage is a necessity; there must not even be a conscious acknowledgment, as it were, of the fact that underlying feelings exist. The cortical action of rechanneling feelings into symbols (symbolic dreams) is part of the entire repressive-defensive system of keeping Primal feelings from becoming conscious Pains.

Although Torda and I would agree on some of the basic neural processes, our interpretations of the meaning of

[3] *Op. cit.*, p. 43.
[4] *Op. cit.*, p. 44.

these processes diverge. She believes that dreams are a "necessary and sufficient condition for programming the brain," [5] while I think they serve a different function; that they are perceptions of *already encoded* memories. Her work is well worth examining. She indicates that dreams contain both short-term and long-term memory traces; in Primal terms, what happens to us during the day triggers off associated old memories. What is important about her work is that she has identified through electrophysiologic evidence significant brain structures involved in this process.

In biochemical terms, Torda sees dreams as a combination of the action of serotonin and norepinephrine. Norepinephrine release induces alerting by activating aspects of the reticular activating system. When theta activity is low and dreams begin (if the content is frightening enough), there may be panic and an increase in norepinephrine output to maintain alerting and repression. Understanding the combination of these two chemical processes may eventually clarify the manic-depressive waking cycle—of total repression and "acting-in" and the subsequent release of energy and "acting-out." In any case, when we relax, there seems to be less inhibition—or, conversely, less inhibition *allows* relaxation.

In neurotics, this lack of inhibition means the time has come for more cortical defense activity so that the mind thinks about other matters; while awake, it may be business, while asleep, symbolic dreams.

The process of repression is mediated by any number of neurochemical agents. But the brain follows a constant method; so repression, whether one is awake or asleep, involves the same structures and same neurochemical changes. When we repress feelings, we become *unconscious* of them, just as the repression of consciousness produces the unconsciousness of sleep. There are many ways to be unconscious, as Freud pointed out many decades ago. When one looks at electroencephalographic (EEG) tracings of very repressed persons and those in deep sleep (both are unconscious states), one usually finds high amplitude waves. As our research indicates, when repression lessens in Primal patients, amplitude can drop by half. In this sense, the neurotic is truly unconscious and kept that way by Pain. No matter how hard he tries to be "aware," Pain will see that he is not. In EEG terms, continuous high-amplitude waves may mean that a person is so unconscious that he cannot effectively differentiate inside from outside. "Inside" suffuses "outside." The result may be psychotic delusions or a bad dream which totally envelops us or, more subtly, the inability to be objective—to see reality for what it is. Being overwhelmed by feelings so that one can no longer differentiate inner from outer means that one is condemned to live in his dream continuously.

So we see there is a subterranean life composed of Primal feelings which spreads as repression mounts and increasingly directs consciousness. One's hold on outside reality depends on how much consciousness is enveloped by the unconscious, by our integration of inside reality.[6]

Because there is little dreaming during deep sleep, the brain is more susceptible to stimulation. There is a higher evoked electrical potential to a stimulus, since there is less brain activity to ward off the input. During D-sleep, however, the brain is quite busy and sensory input is warded off. In EEG terms, this may mean that a person with a slower brain frequency is more open to what is going on outside him; he is more aware. Being a feeling person, then, means (in EEG terms) to be open to stimulation—open to the world.

[6] Later, in the research section, I will discuss how we have begun to measure degrees of repression and neurosis and how brain-wave studies are opening new insights to our understanding of sleeptime neurosis. Briefly, we think that there is a relationship of amplitude to brain-wave frequency. As the brain slows down in sleep one gets closer to his unconscious feelings, and to protect against them more neurons are recruited for suppression, resulting in higher amplitudes. By simulating aspects of sleep through pulsing the brain with strobe lights so that it slows considerably, we have found that in feeling people there are Primals, and in unfeeling neurotics there is a surge of repressive force and a commensurate rise in amplitude.

With brain-wave patterns part of the defense system, changes in sleep waves provide us with a relatively uncontaminated index of therapeutic progress.

The ninety-minute cycle occurs with or without neurosis, in my opinion. With neurosis, the buildup and release of tension is greatly increased because the reservoir of tension is so much greater. Perhaps a more precise description of the D-state is that it is an alert-release period. In this sense, the system mobilizes itself for defense against danger in ninety-minute cycles, day and night, and then releases itself from this vigilance into a defenseless, relaxed state. In normal persons who have no reservoir of Primal Pain, the release may simply be moving about during the day—exercising, stretching, or whatever. At night, it may take the form of real dreams.

To tamper with neurotic defenses is unwise particularly if the tension which drives these defenses cannot be reduced by proper physical and mental connections. To remove the defense, to put the person on a crash diet or stop his smoking completely, is to raise the tension level, producing more disturbed sleep. And indeed a late research finding on smokers who stopped abruptly found just that—more disturbed sleep and more possibility of coronary attack.

Evidence for the defensive nature of the D-states is found in cats who, while asleep and in this state, can walk around, prowl, and attack invisible enemies. The fact that these periods are basic and not just dream events is attested to by research with cats who have had their cortex removed. Deprived surgically of any ability to dream, they still experience their D-state cycles.[7] In other words, the D-state—what I would term an arousal or vigilant, defensive time—is an ancient phylogenetic legacy, part of an inbuilt survival mechanism common to almost all animal life. It occurred even before the development of a complex human cortex.

Just how all this relates to research on mental illness is shown in a study by Dement (1964). He found an abnormally high D-time in schizophrenics in remission; that

[7] See the extensive research by M. Jouvet on this point.

is, the more adjusted or "well" the person could act during the day, the more his night life was disturbed. D-time and mental illness work like a hydraulic system; the more there is of one, the less is necessary of the other. More precisely, mental illness *is* D-states which have broken out into one's waking life.

Hartmann cites one longitudinal study of a paranoid patient who had a 30 percent D-time while in remission and a 50 percent D-time as he began again slipping into his paranoia. He guardedly concluded that there was a relationship between D-time and drive pressure leading to psychotic illness. The implication is that neurotic release forms are defenses against insanity.

Hartmann cites a study by Koranyi and Lehmann (1960) indicating that psychotics were more sensitive to sleep deprivation than normal subjects. One hundred hours of sleep deprivation in these persons resulted in a return of each patient's psychotic symptoms—symptoms that had not shown up for months or years. Furthermore, patients who can normally recall their dreams mention that they "ceased dreaming" during episodes of mental illness. Further evidence indicates that brain discharges associated with petit mal epilepsy decrease during D-periods except for those caused by scars from previous brain injury. D-states, then, can act as a lever in some cases of epilepsy, lowering petit mal discharge states. Depressives have a greater amount of D-time than manic-acting neurotics. If one acts in, therefore, more disturbed sleep is produced than if one is able to act out during the day. There is research evidence to validate this point.[8] Experimental subjects who were completely socially isolated for one day had an average of 60 percent more dream time during the night—evidence again that dreams release tension. I would doubt, for instance, that one would see such an increase in dreaming in normals who were socially isolated.

It is commonplace for Primal patients who have had interrupted Primals in their homes (because of visitors, for example) to suffer severe nightmares during the same night. The nightmare *is* the leftover feeling from the

[8] Charles T. Tart, *Altered States of Consciousness* (New York: Wiley, 1969), p. 140.

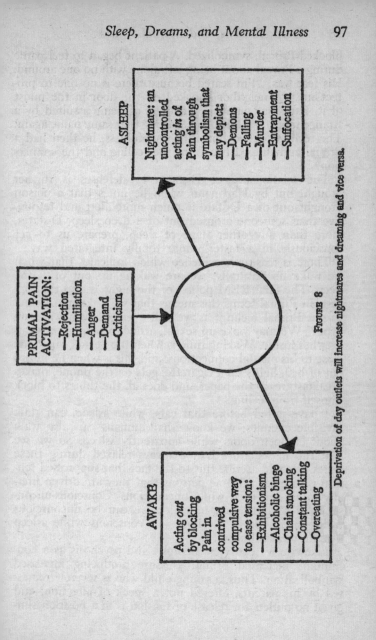

PRIMAL PAIN ACTIVATION:
—Rejection
—Humiliation
—Anger
—Demand
—Criticism

ASLEEP

Nightmare; an uncontrolled acting *in* of Pain through symbolism that may depict:
—Demons
—Falling
—Murder
—Entrapment
—Suffocation

AWAKE

Acting *out* by blocking Pain in contrived compulsive way to ease tension:
—Exhibitionism
—Alcoholic binge
—Chain smoking
—Constant talking
—Overeating

FIGURE 8

Deprivation of day outlets will increase nightmares and dreaming and vice versa.

blocked Primal, symbolized. A patient began to feel panic during a Primal about being left alone with no one around. His fear was: "I'm scared because there is no one to protect me." A neighbor knocked on the door in the midst of it. Late that night, he dreamed of being assulted by a strange monster while alone, feeling that same panic again. The feeling pushed him into wakefulness; he then had a Primal and slipped back into the feeling and the connection.

The relationship of D-states to defenses is further brought out by Hartmann when he notes that a person brought out of a D-state is much more alert and responsive than someone aroused out of a deep sleep. D-states, more than any other stage of sleep, prepare us to act consciously in a faster, more totally integrated way.

There is reasearch evidence which indicates that when we wake up naturally, we are waking up out of REM sleep. The final REM period of the night is also the longest. In Primal terms this means that we wake up as close to our Primal feelings as we will ever get: you wake up "you." We may wake up sexual, afraid, or angry, or whatever lies inside. Waking time is when the person can come close to his mental connections, and this is when he jumps out of bed, lights up a cigarette, gets on the phone, makes breakfast, reads the paper, and does all the things to block himself from feeling.

I have noted before that cats, while asleep, can stalk invisible enemies; we know that humans can also walk about or open doors while apparently asleep. So we see that the masculature is not always relaxed during these states. I would ascribe this to the fact that suppressed tension is so great in some persons that they are driven literally to act out even while unconscious. Conscious-unconscious is a continuum in which we can be unconscious while awake—as in psychosis—or conscious while asleep —as in somnambulism.

Likewise we can view neurosis and psychosis as a continuum: increased Primal pressure producing increased symbolization. Thus, a young child who is severely repressed by his parents, offered not a speck of affection, and given no outlets for release of tension is in a position similar to the adult neurotic deprived of sleep (and dreams) for a long period of time. In both cases the accumulated pressure can easily lead to bizarre psychotic ideation.

Dreams must take up the slack for tension release. Take away food and cigarettes which have been used to tranquilize the system, and the body reacts much as if medical tranquilizers have been suddenly removed. The end result is the rebound. Similarly, one could hypothesize that alcoholics and drug addicts who have been suddenly withdrawn from their habits suffer from more bad dreams and nightmares; the system must make up for the loss of daytime tranquilization.

Someone deprived of his daytime outlets, even when that deprivation occurs under the aegis of professionals who call it "conditioning," say, must find some way to release the accumulated tension. Bad dreams are one way. And bad dreams for the addict deprived of his drugs mean that tension continues its assualt, until at some later time a severe physical symptom can result. The warning signs are those tense dreams, and the amount of drugs necessary for sound sleep will depend on the amount of Pain. It is interesting to note that children tolerate much smaller doses of drugs than adults, even of aspirins. Medical men have believed that this is largely due to differences in body weight, but may it not be due too to children's less viscous defense systems?

To reiterate the basic premise: Any event which can be felt and integrated is a real, feeling experience. Any load beyond the integration point which cannot be connected is diverted into symbolic channels such as in dreams. Overload is the "stuff" of symbolic dreams; the energy of unintegrated feeling determines the emotional power of the dream. A simple criticism as an adult would produce no overload, by and large, if that criticism were not tied to earlier rejections in life. The *combined* force is what creates the overload. The solution is not found in the analysis of the manifest content of the dream; it is in helping the person slowly reintegrate the overload.

As an overload lessens we see a dual phenomenon. In homosexuals, for example, we will see the first heterosexual dreams and, simultaneously, the first inklings of heterosexual interest. The dream foreshadows that will later emerge as a fully conscious heterosexuality. As a man deals with his fear of his mother and feels: "Why didn't you ever want me?" his dream content will change accordingly and less frightening female characters will appear in them. Again we see that change is automatic and unconscious. A person begins to change his sexual orientation without deliberate, conscious will. Until those feelings are felt, defending against them will be automatic and unconscious, so that homosexuality will be a matter of course. The person may not be aware of any terror of females while awake, but with less conscious guard during sleep, the real feelings (though not connected to their proper source) will emerge.

One reason dreams are important is that they are portents of what is to come. When the underlying blocked feelings begin having access to conscious, the key way-station is dream life. That is how we know when a neurotic is close to his feelings: he suffers from bad dreams. A person totally repressed may have no recognition of his dream life at all. As feelings finally reach consciousness, they seem to leave the subterranean cavern for good; they are no longer unconscious forces which can produce nightmares.

We can understand nightmares better by examining the LSD experience. LSD artificially floods the cortex with Primal feelings (through disinhibition of inhibitory centers); a person begins living his nightmare. Afterward, if he can regain his defenses (if the Pain is not shattering), he might well say, "My God, I am out of that nightmare!" If he cannot reconstitute his neurotic defenses, he will become entangled in the symbolic labyrinth and lose touch with reality.

Symbolizing should be seen as a crucial form of release. We all have had the experience of being angry at someone and not saying what we feel. We then may daydream our revenge. If we stopped the person from daydreaming, we would produce increased pressure because we have shut off the feeling totally. There is a school of therapy called Directed Daydreaming in which patients are encouraged to create symbolic situations and act out their fantasies.

They will pretend they are crawling through a tunnel to freedom, for example, and state that they feel better for a while. They have managed to do what a good dream does—focus and release tension symbolically. Delusions are also necessary to the psychic equilibrium of someone in great Pain. If a person suffering from psychosomatic disease were encouraged to fantasize and act out those fantasies safely, it could be an effective tension-draining approach, albeit only a temporary expedient.

In summary, dream research thus far indicates that humans must release tension, and neurotics must release neurotic tension. Dreams are not different phenomena from waking behavior, but the same essential process. Neurosis permits release of tension and guards against psychosis. Prohibiting neurosis day or night leaves the person susceptible to psychosis. Primal drive pressure mounts when release forms are deprived, causing correlated increased symbolic behavior both quantitatively and qualitatively. Nothing can stop Primal tension other than connection, and danger to the organism occurs when neurotic outlets are prevented either through the use of drugs or through social inhibition. Symbolic dreams are the neurosis in neurotics just as nightmares are the psychosis that occurs when usual neurotic outlets cannot do the job. Finally, dreams are no more than the symbolic images and ideation driven by feelings, just as any bizarre ideas occur when feelings are blocked.

III. The Birth Primal

1. INTRODUCTION

Nowhere is the existence of reverberating memory circuits more dramatically illustrated than in the birth Primal—the reliving of traumas which occurred before we entered the world. These traumas were registered in the system before any consciousness developed to interpret and analyze them. They have eluded us in psychotherapy up to now because psychotherapy has been largely an analytic mode. Birth Primals have been videotaped and filmed. Hundreds of them have been observed, and their forms and intensity leave little question as to their reality.

The brain overloads not only in response to terrible external realities—psychologic events such as the death of a parent—but also from a catastrophic physical trauma such as birth. The unresolved event lays down its great load of tension thereafter. It drives behavior, helps shape future ideas, and plays a significant part in subsequent symptom formation. The severity of the symptom or the irrationality of the idea formed later will be commensurate with the amount of tension in the system. A most traumatic birth may produce or contribute to a most severe physical symptom later on. The Primal excess causes excessive drive or behavior later—extra loud speech, eating too much, talking too much, shopping too much, etc.

The significance of catastrophic early traumas is that they become a focal point or prototype of later behavior. It is not limited to birth trauma; circumcision can be just as traumatic. Later in life, under general threat, a person may react with a pain or cutting sensation in his penis. Even a minor situation later in life can reactivate the early prototypic trauma and produce a disproportionate reaction. Physical trauma can fixate a child and help determine how he will react to later stress.

Not all births are traumatic, but given a neurotic world with neurotic mothers it is very difficult to avoid pain at birth. This can be caused by excessively long labor owing to a mother's rigidly shutting down against pain, or by accidental factors, such as breech birth, strangulation by the cord, pinched cord, pain caused by harsh use of forceps, and so on.

The psychologic literature overlooks the fact that the birth process represents a relationship between mother and child, a relationship in which the child is learning. A difficult birth "teaches" the child that he is helpless against overwhelming odds, that he is powerless to change things, that life is dangerous and a struggle. These are emotional teachings, but they become the matrix for future learning; thus a person may come later to believe in the necessity of struggle as a sine qua non of life. He unconsciously is rationalizing the need for struggle in order to live because that was his birth experience. The fact that it is not conscious does not alter the fact that it was a personal experience which shapes ideas and attitudes. To try to change that person's philosophy would be tantamount to talking him out of his history.

Evidence of the way birth traumas shape later behavior was dramatically illustrated in the birth Primal of a patient whose head was stuck at birth and suffered from an enforced rotation while still in the canal. After reliving this trauma he ceased his subtle tic of moving his head from side to side whenever he spoke.

Neurosis can begin in the womb, and especially during the birth process. For example, a trait such as always deferring to the wants of others might seem to be caused by the mother's constant refrain: "Quiet! What will the neighbors think?" Or because children constantly had to defer to their father's moods and whims when he came home from work. We usually can find ample evidence in the interaction of the family to account for the reasons a child must acquiesce to others and defer his own needs. But the *prototype* of an acquiescent response may begin during the birth process with a mother who cannot tolerate pain and therefore holds back on releasing the child into the world. The natural rhythmical process of birth has been interrupted; the neonate no longer "senses" a natural rhythm in which he is being helped by his mother

—instead he must *defer* his own natural rhythm (his own self) to her neurosis. He is already out of rhythm with himself by the time he is born. The fact that he must begin life acquiescing may help determine how he will later react to mother's caution about what the neighbors will think. If he did not begin life acquiescing, if he had to struggle aggressively to get out, he may later react aggressively and defiantly to mother's caution instead of deferring to her.

Let us take being born out of rhythm and see what sequelae might result. If a great deal of stress is laid on speech, making the child speak early, then the focus of the disharmony laid down at birth may result in sporadic, arhythmical stammering or halting speech—a nonfluid speech, the predisposition for which began with a nonfluid birth process. The traumatic birth process becomes "frozen" and encapsulated in the organism, maintained in its entirety because it is an unresolved event. Aspects of the trauma, such as disharmony, become focused in areas of vulnerability (organically weak areas, resulting in unpredictable menstrual flow or sporadic bowel function and constipation), or in areas of special psychological stress such as speech. That disharmony could just as easily result in a nonfluid gait if walking were stressed before the child was ready. In other words, the inability to integrate that experience causes a lack of integration or coordination between thought and speech or between thought and physical ability.

We know from the extensive literature on circadian rhythms that nearly all life processes follow a natural rhythm—temperature, menstruation, dreams, etc. The need to be in one's own rhythm is a basic one, perhaps as important as any other Primal need. When we talk about making a child speak or walk prematurely we are discussing an interference with natural rhythm. For evolution is a rhythm—a time of ebb and flow—a time for readiness of function and a time of cessation of function (such as menstruation). I believe a speech disorder would not result unless there were numerous overloads in the area of speech. That is, birth disharmony might not result in overt stammering speech unless added to that birth trauma was an *additional disharmony* or disruption in natural rhythm by making the child speak before he was ready. The combined trauma result in a symptom. Conversely, symptoms are indications that the body is overloaded and cannot smoothly integrate its experience.

Arhythmicity is something learned in a relationship between the neonate and the mother, just as many things are "learned" in nonconceptual ways very early in life or when life begins.

I call the initial catastrophic event, whether birth trauma, circumcision, etc., the Prototype Primal Trauma. The early overload situation fixates the infant so that his response to that trauma becomes fixed and stable, causing a similar response to later trauma. It is as though that overload event becomes a central repository for all similar traumas which are connected to each other neurologically and stored together. Waiting to get out of the womb is an example. Any situation in which the child is made to wait later on, not being allowed to go to the toilet when the urge hits him, say, will become attached to the original birth trauma and may reactivate the *entire unit* or experiences. That explains why after a brith Primal experience in therapy a patient will be deluged with insights and memories; the whole filing cabinet of pain comes up for connection and integration. So much comes up that it cannot be entirely integrated, which is why there is the Primal Epoch—the week or two or three of constant Primals after the initial birth Primal with all the various connections and insights.

Clearly, there are many kinds of early traumas. A birth trauma can be followed by inadequate breast feeding, for example, so the person is traumatized by birth and then again traumatized by inadequate sucking. Each trauma shapes his personality. The need to suck coupled with later deprivation of father's love may eventually turn into homosexuality, and the need to suck penises. Homosexuality will be reversed only when *each* connected trauma —the need for father, the need to suck, etc.—is relived and resolved in Primal Therapy. Until the majority of connections are made, until the shift is made from predominatly unreal to predominantly real, homosexuality (or homosexual tendencies) will persist. The notion that we can urge (or even punish) a homosexual to "go straight" by having numerous affairs with the opposite sex neglects a lifetime history.

The notion of Prototypic Primal Trauma and its companion, Prototypic Defense, is important in understanding later neurotic responses to stress. Let us speculate that owing to congestion by fluids in the birth canal (or just after birth) the neonate was traumatized so that the only way he could save his own life was reflexively to constrict his bronchioles. The anxiety and the defense now become frozen in time so that any later stress stiuation which may be interpreted as life-endangering—a violent argument between the child's parents, threatening divorce and dissolution of the home—will automatically set off the initial life-saving response of bronchiole constriction. The result may be an asthmatic attack (given certain hereditary predispositions which never should be neglected in any discussion of symptoms), and instead of the organism's being saved it is in danger of death. The bronchiole defense occurs because the life-threatening argument sets off the *original* threat of death coming out of the birth canal, *and* the original physical response. In the case of intrinsic asthma, we can say only that a cure exists when the patient has relived and resolved the original prototypic anxiety situation (the major Primal Scene) which set that particular response in motion.

The prototypic trauma establishes the characteristic mode of defense. If the initial trauma was circumcision, later threats *may* set off impotence or avoidance of the use of the penis. It would take much more than circumcision alone to cause impotence, but that trauma may have a directive effect in subsequent situations of fear. Circumcision plus fear of mother may produce impotence when a man is in a sexual situation with an aggressive, domineering woman.

The term "directive" is important, for great early trauma can set the direction of one's life. Recently, a woman in therapy came into the office feeling suicidal. She kept saying, "I don't want to live. I don't want to live!" After screaming about all the current problems she had, she fell into a birth Primal, writhing and thrashing for half an hour. She came out of it with the insight that from the time of birth she sensed she was not wanted. The birth trauma coming up initially aroused an inchoate feeling of not wanting to live—back when she was born owing to the struggle and agony of birth. The insight that followed revealed that most of her life she had become involved with people who did not want her. She was always the aggressor with her boyfriends, calling them up and asking if she could come over for a while. She maneuvered her life so that she did not give anyone time to want her. She wouldn't take a chance on feeling not wanted—the early "not wanted." The prototypic trauma, combined with having a mother who did not want her, then, *directed* her behavior thereafter. She spent a lifetime finding rejecting people with whom she could struggle to make them want her.

Whether a person automatically has an asthma attack later on in feeling-provoking situations or feels compelled to cruise for homosexual contacts, it means he is stuck in the symbolic-neurotic stage. Instead of feeling: "I'm being drowned by birth fluid" or: "I have no real daddy," the person blocks the painful feeling and engages in automatic symbolic behavior.

There are two ways we can get to prototypic feelings in Primal Therapy. We can reawaken the memory verbally by having a patient describe early scenes; or we can reawaken a preverbal memory physically by stimulating the early scene. At the appropriate time in therapy we can put wet towels over the mouth and nose of a patient to simulate suffocation or butt the person's head against a pillow or a wall. The aim, verbal or preverbal, is to elicit early memory circuits.

One of the ways we see fixated defenses manifested is in bad dreams or nightmares. The early trauma is preserved in pure form, arising in the dream only slightly disguised. For example, being suffocated at birth has resulted in nightmares of drowning or of being enclosed in rooms without air. Being squeezed at birth has resulted in dreams of being stuck in a tunnel or mine shaft. In other words, the exact traumatic sensations of pain at birth arise in the dream wrapped in symbolic ideation. If a person knew that those sensations were the exact birth sensations, he might (assuming he were open enough) transmute that dream into an actual birth sequence.

The progressive, subtle traumas involving the daily interpersonal relationships between parent and child help complicate the basic birth dream and add extra symbolism to the dream. The recurrent bad dream is instructive because a person can dream about being stuck underground in a tunnel, or of being drowned, year after year and never produce a "good" ending to that dream. Why? Because the *feeling* and sensations must be connected and resolved exactly as they occurred, when they occurred. There cannot be a good ending so long as the trauma of being suffocated at birth resides as a memory unit in the brain, innervating the entire system, producing recurrent dreams.

Recurrent dreams may occur in response to *any* threat felt as life-threatening. One need not be suffocating in a stuffy bedroom to have the initial suffocating feeling return in the form of a dream; it may be set off by being symbolically suffocated by someone's towering, domineering presence.

As I have already noted, dreams often foreshadow the ascending feeling. As a patient progresses in Primal Therapy we sometimes have an idea of what is about to occur by examining the patient's dream life. One patient came in on a Saturday telling of a dream in which he was walking down an ever narrowing corridor until he was stuck and could not move. He had never had this dream before. On the following Monday, he complained of being stuck in his therapy and not getting anywhere. He did not connect the complaint with his dream. We simulated a birth canal and stuck his head in it, allowing his head to butt against the end. Within minutes he was in a birth Primal. After he came out of it he said, "I have often felt stuck in my life like 'I couldn't make it.' I attached that feeling of not being able to make it to other things—school, marriage, therapy, and so on. I see now that it all started when my life started, when I almost didn't make it."

If we had put this man's head in a simulated canal in the first weeks of therapy, nothing would have happened.

He was not ready for such a catastrophic feeling. As he became ready, crucial signs appeared, particularly in his dreams. The dream was never analyzed, only noted for future reference.

This process is even more complex than it seems. This man had many previous Primals over the feeling: "I can't make it without you, Daddy." These Primals occured after he was let down by his committee chairman in graduate school. When the chairman failed to fight for him, he had the Primal about his father. He then discovered that he had always looked for a strong man to lead the way for him; to talk for him, get dates for him, etc. But underlying this feeling of "I can't make it" was the prototypic birth feeling. Perhaps a strong father in his life would have been a great enough force to conteract the power of the birth trauma. A strong father who encouraged him would have counteracted the influence of the prototypic trauma and prevented that trauma from interfering with his later performance. For instance, he might not have dropped out of school when the going got tough. But the underlying prototypic force would always be a latent potential; if the father died, the potential might become a reality. Without the father to say, "You can make it. Let me help you," a demanding school situation might provoke the early feeling of "I can't make it" and cause him to drop out of school. We can begin to understand that later behavior is a result of Primal forces and countervailing forces (a good teacher, living in the same house for decades, an encouraging father, a helpful brother, etc.). Those forces hold the Primal ones in check; they do not eradicate them. They may, however, prevent the outbreak of symptoms —such as learning disabilities, school failure, etc.

Before Primal Therapy, the man discussed above had many dreams of trying to get the class and *never being able to make it*—he couldn't find the room number, he was too late for class, and so on. Early school trauma, then, became the focus (the story theme) for the prototypic feeling. Others have continuing dreams of not ever reaching their destination, not being able to get the car started, not being able to swim back to shore, etc.—all derivative, possibly, of the early trauma.

Another related feeling in neurotics when under stress is: "Something terrible is going to happen." A teacher in class will call on them and they will have that instant doomed feeling. Why? Again the academic situation may be connected to the prototypic one. Something terrible *did happen* to us very early in life. Only we don't know what it is. But later threat makes us feel that very real feeling. Psychotherapists often consider that doomed feeling as neurotic because, they point out, "Nothing catastrophic did happen when the teacher asked us to report in front of the class." They fail to understand that the doomed, something-terrible-is-going-to-happen feeling is a response to a real, but buried, event.

We have labeled people "neurotic" because we have failed to understand the context to which they are responding. Their responses are *real*. So-called neurotic reactions are *appropriate* reactions to shattering situations, situations which are a mystery to both the therapist and the patient. Only the unconscious system of the patient "knows" what it is. Once we understand that neurotics are reacting to an unresolved past projected onto the present the mystery of neurosis evaporates.

We have been most fortunate for the first time in history to have adults making conscious reports of their birth. What they have to say should be heeded by physicians who bring children into this world. For example, drugging the mother during birth. A number of patients reported going "numb" during the later part of the birth Primal; they feel sure they absorbed some of the mother's anesthetic. Instead of coming into this world alive and bouncy, active participants in a joyous occasion, they slip into the world half-conscious and numb. Patients then say that they later go "numb" under stress. Certainly great hesitation should be urged before using any drugs on a mother in labor. I think that part of the reason we drug mothers is the same reason we drug so many other adults—we cannot take "hysterical" outbursts in others without feeling personal panic. A quieter mother is probably less trouble for the doctor.

Permitting long labor is another terrible trauma for the neonate, for he arrives on this earth depleted of his energy and reserves. Reacting exhausted to later trauma is one example of this Prototypic Primal Anxiety. Being thus depleted is not a simple temporary state, it turns out; the neonate may react later in his infancy as though he did not have energy enough to cope with situations—not "aggressive enough," some mothers call it.

A patient who suffered from epileptic seizures for years recently came into therapy. During the first week of treatment he went into a birth Primal in which he felt his head crashing against something; after two hours he began wailing like a newborn. He later explained that his was a very hard and long labor and that his mother told him he came out wailing. (This was later confirmed by his mother.) The impact of the pressure on his head in trying to get born may not have been physiologically traumatic, but it certainly was the focal point of a psychlogical trauma. After a few months of life left alone in the crib without being fed or picked up he began head-banging against the end of his crib. In his teens seizure activity began.

Since the day he entered therapy, his seizures have been rare, despite the fact that he took no Dilantin from his first day. What does this mean? For one thing, the tension set up *at birth* was significant in terms of its *overall* contribution to his general tension level later on. The high level of tension would spill over into an epileptic symptom, focused in the key area of his early trauma, much in the same way as patients develop a skin rash under adult stress —that is, they develop a symptom in the area of early trauma so that any later stress situation, even one unrelated to the focal area (skin, head etc.), produces the fixated response.

If the epiletic had had a decent early life, he could have had a birth trauma and never developed epileptic symptoms. It is my observation, however, that birth traumas carry a large valence in their contribution to the general level of chronic tension. This is partly owing to the organism's newness and fragility in terms of its ability to cope with stress and, most importantly, because birth traumas are often matters of life and death— a neonate strangling on the umbilical cord will really die unless something is done. Thus a life-and-death struggle takes place with many of us even before we come into this world.

One other example. Recently, a woman came to therapy because of a lifetime of "pressure headaches," as she called them. In her second month of therapy she underwent a birth Primal which I supervised. For two and one-half hours she was curled in a ball, spitting up fluid and butting her head against the (padded) wall. The butting process was clearly automatic and involuntary, and it is doubtful that anyone could continue to butt her head against a wall for more than two hours without exhaustion. Her head twisted and turned constantly. She explained later that she was "trying to get out." She discovered days later that she had undergone an unusually long labor. That trauma became the prototype of a specific reaction pattern; namely, that under any later stress she would develop a "pressure headache." Neither she nor I ever could have guessed the origin of her headaches; if we were to try to understand her symptom within the conventional analytic mode, we could have posited guilt over not having sufficiently helped her sick mother, suppressed anger at her father, and so on—all of which could be true. But those would not explain how guilt or anger becomes transmuted into a headache which puts a person in bed for days.

The best proof of the origin of her headaches is the fact that after this birth Primal she no longer had pressure headaches. Her husband told me later that when he touched her neck it felt "soft and pliant" for the first time since he could remember. Electromyograph studies of her neck muscles one day after the birth Primal produced a reading of very low tension.

All of this does not mean that she could not have developed headaches based on suppressed anger. However, it is my observation that the *severity* of the symptom is commensurate with the severity of the trauma. A few aspirins might assuage some guilt or anger but would be powerless against the pressure of the birth trauma. This woman could have a birth Primal only after "preparing" herself through experiencing many lesser Primals before-hand. Her body, drained of lesser Pains, lifted the load to the degree that she could now integrate such a major Pain as birth.

Once her body was ready for that experience, it began to ascend on its own without any conscious effort or planning by the patient; it was relentless.

The day that the birth Primal began to emerge in the woman discussed above, she began having terrible pressure headaches as soon as she awoke in the morning. She knew she had to get into the office as soon as possible, started to drive her car, and blacked out. Luckily she called for aid and someone brought her in to us, where she had her Primal. Had she never had Primal Therapy, a merciful defense system would constantly keep her away from that Primal by converting it into amorphous tension which she could smoke or drink away, or somatize in the form of headaches and blackouts and dizziness.

Not every person needs to go through a birth Primal. Those who do have the experience often make leaps in their therapy. It is as though that Primal has been a dam against feeling anything else, and once opened, the whole system is flooded with Primals thereafter. After birth Primals, as we shall demonstrate, there are sharp drops in core body temperature as well as other measurements, corroborative evidence of the amount of chronic bodily tension generated by the birth trauma.

It would seem that during traumatic birth the organism splits *right then* (from feeling fully) so that further psychologic traumas only widen the split. When the organism splits at birth, there is often a "dead" quality to the person's personality thereafter. The reason for the lifelessness is that at no time in this world was the person totally himself and feeling.

When feelings are split off from consciousness at birth hormone balance can be affected because hormones mediate feelings. What appears to be genetic hormonal imbalances in infants much more likely may be the result of birth processes, not heredity. An infant suffering hypothyroidism may come from an ancestry with predispositions to low thyroid output, but the triggering mechanism which produced the disease may be the initial birth trauma.

Integration of birth traumas in Primal Therapy seems to corroborate the above point, for radical changes take place in these patients in terms of their hormone structure. Hypothyroidism (when the damage has not been too severe) has changed and become normal in some of these patients. An integrated system means that the entire interactory nature of the hormone system changes, resulting in a greater fluidity and proper balance. Hair texture, skin texture, sex drive, and breast size change. Hair distribution changes as well. Women who were quite hairy become less so; and men who could not grow beards enjoy much fuller growth. Protein-bound iodine tests indicate significant changes in thyroid function.

Perhaps it should be stated at this point that patients who have undergone birth Primals rarely had anticipated the experience or even knew that such a thing was possible. The same can be said for circumcision Primals. It is most difficult, if not impossible, to fake such an experience. On film one can see the remarkable similarity in birth Primals—the fetal position, hands turned in, eyes rolled back, the roll of the head and the lack of words during the experience; just grunts and groans, not even the baby cry.

Patients who were choked on birth fluid will often bring up rivers of mucus during the Primal. Often any Primal (nonbirth) will cause them to begin spitting up, and they will not stop this process until they relive the prototypic trauma. After that they do not spit up again. Indeed after this kind of Primal patients who have suffered from chest congestion for years will find themselves feeling clear inside. In this sense, a congested chest or dripping nose is a symbolic manifestation of Primal events; once the events are connected to consciousness they stop having an *unconscious* effect. Just because the symbolic behavior was physical does not make it any less symbolic. Allergies are real, but the reality of an allergy is not so much dust and pollen as the event which produced the initial sensitivity.

Let us discuss allergies for a moment. There is no doubt of a hereditary predisposition for allergic reactions, but the steps from heredity to an actual running nose are complex. Perhaps the fetus was battered and bruised during birth, and the patient may later develop a general sensitivity which can take several forms. If he has no physical predisposition to allergy, he may become sensitive to being bruised. One patient, for example, was a breech birth, born with his arms broken. In later life, anyone who brushed up against him harshly set off this sensitivity to hurt. He was ready to smash those people so that they could not hurt him anymore—fighting was a defense against feeling the early hurt.

But if the same person had a systemic sensitivity, under later stress he would have a sensitivity (allergic) reaction. He would begin life battered and then would be battered psychologically during his early years until he could no longer take it, at which point he would develop allergies. Often a triggering event pushes his over the threshold into symptoms. Perhaps his mother was taken to a hospital for several months or his father got a new job and had to leave for a prolonged period. Once the allergic reaction sets in, the symptoms may be triggered by various noxious stimulants including dust and pollen. The pollen does not *cause* the allergy (and sensitivity shots do not cure it); it triggers it. If the person has a settled life situation, it will take more noxious stimuli to set off his allergy. If he has a ligh level of tension, it may take less to activate it.

During the "birth" period, patients report occasional incontinence. They have to urinate frequently and often "dribble" small amounts periodically. They sometimes seem clumsy, will fall down easily, and and cannot balance objects in their hands. Speaking becomes difficult. They are not totally "out of it," but these all form minor annoyances. Other patients report that their skin peels—and we can see it happening. Others find that their clothes feel heavy—and one patient reported that her hair felt heavy, after having been born bald. I won't go on because I am sure it already seems bizarre enough. But the point is that the brain and body *preserve* nonintegrated experience in its *exact form* for a lifetime.

One of the more dramatic documentations of the way infantile trauma is preserved intact is shown in the case of a patient whose birthmark returned when she began having birth Primals. A bright-red strawberry mark appeared on her chest and lasted for weeks. Where was that mark all the preceding years? We can only assume that the entire birth experience and its sequela were an encapsulated memory circuit until it was set off in therapy.

One final point about the way psychotic phenomena such as delusions relate to birth traumas. Birth traumas are nonconceptual, undifferentiated pains. A person carrying this load will try to focus or pinpoint the source of his misery; he may develop a delusion in an effort to conceptualize this nonconceptual hurt. Catastrophic birth traumas may later produce a susceptibility to serious mental illness because the initial split began when life began; there were not enough years without pain to permit viable defenses to develop.

We see what a wonder the human system is. Under stress the body returns to its time and areas of damage in an effort to repair itself. The miracle is that we can go back forty and fifty years and undo traumas which occurred then, traumas which shaped our lives and helped form our later ideas.

Our neglect of prototypic traumas has caused an inability to understand how symptoms begin, and how the vicious neurotic cycle gets its start. A child held back at birth is immediately irritable and tense. He demands more from his mother, who in turn becomes impatient with him and angry at his demands. She's cross and he's all the more upset. He enters school tense and unable to sit still and concentrate. For this he gets more disapproval. He becomes a "problem" child—and so the cycle goes. A mother who keeps her baby in a long labor is setting a pattern of relationship. It isn't as though the mother is one way at birth and another later on. The birth relationship is part of what kind of mother she will be. The birth process foreshadows the neurotic parent-child relationship to come.

We now have a frame of reference to understand the

ways in which we develop symptoms. Thus far in psychology we have been preoccupied with categorizing symptoms, hoping that such categories would lead to deeper comprehension. We see now why one symptom is chosen over another. One woman, for example, found herself less and less frigid as she had Primals about the sexual attitudes of her parents. But her frigidity remained until she had a prototypic Primal about constantly being bound too tightly with a diaper so that it caused pain (and constriction) around her vagina. Vaginal constriction was a prototypic defense; it became a problem of frigidity because of the overlay of puritanical parental attitudes.

We may now understand why one person with puritanical parents becomes frigid while another with the same kind of parents does not. We see why the only expert who can ferret out causes for symptoms is the patient—and his Primal experiences. What has seemed to be genetic disease may be much more a function of prototypic traumas. For example, manic-depressive psychosis, or the "cyclic" personality, has been long considered a genetic proclivity. One patient was delayed in birth for two weeks and then born in a rush. During a Primal he had the insight that his cyclic behavior and his up-and-down moods began with being "out of synch" at birth. No therapist would dare make such an insight connection for the patient; yet this patient *knew* the validity of such an insight through a Primal experience. The fact that he no longer suffered from diurnal moods added corroboration to his notion. He solved a lifelong problem of feeling "held down" or depressed during the morning and then engaging in manic activity later in the day. He called himself a "night person" for years without understanding its origins.

The epileptic patient began to retard seizures. We will discuss the relationship of his epilepsy to birth trauma later. Suffice to note that before therapy he began having seizures in his sleep. He logged them and noted that they occured about every ninety minutes (see Part II). Connections to those early traumas will end his epileptic nightmare.

Let us now look at birth Primals in the words of those

best qualified to describe them—those who have relived them themselves.

Robert

I entered therapy when I was twenty-three years old, a graduate student in psychology, and a therapist in training. On a friend's suggestion I read *The Primal Scream*. Like most therapists, I wanted to get the best tidbits of the Primal techniques and incorporate them into my eclectic therapeutic stew.

The only flaw in my thinking this time was myself; I was affected by the book so much that I began to have pre-Primals—real feelings of pain. I began to worry about falling apart before I could get into this new therapy which I hoped would put me back together again. Later I found that just like Humpty-Dumpty I couldn't ever be put back together. Once my pain began to surface, it was impossible to maintain a functional neurosis.

I called the Janovs—I now wanted to get well. Vivian (Mrs. Janov) told me, "You can't possibly get into therapy before October and maybe December" (four to seven months away). I neurotically accepted this. The following day Art called me and said, "You have begun Primal Therapy." "When?" I asked. "Now; go to the motel immediately." Someone had canceled and I was taking his place. Whoever you are—I thank you for being so neurotic as to cancel. Within two hours I was driving away from my mountain home into the brown smog of Los Angeles. Dante would have been pleased at the transition from the neurotic tranquillity of the mountains to the hellish atmosphere which I, a long-haired, bearded, hip young therapist was making.

SESSION ONE—Monday

9 A.M. and I begin thinking that Janov and "his highly trained staff" were Beverly Hills quacks who cured country club neurotics. "What am I doing here? I really do powerful therapy myself and I'm not so sick. Fuck, I feel scared and sad."

I entered the office and a curly-haired child named Les

introduced himself to me. "I'm Les, you're Robert."
"Yes." I wanted to know more, and this boy was telling
me that I am Robert. Les told me to lie down. He asked,
"How do you feel?" "Sad."

With this ungodly and simple introduction I began my
descent into my own hell—the seemingly endless corri-
dors of pain. As I went into the sadness a quote came to
me from Joseph Conrad:

> A man that is born falls into a dream like a man who
> falls into the sea. If he tries to climb out into the air
> as inexperienced people endeavor to do, he drowns—
> nicht wahr? No! I tell you! The way is to the destruc-
> tive elements submit yourself. . . . In the destructive
> elements immerse yourself.

I can't say I went into the sadness; it was more like
falling. I began to breathe deeply from my diaphragm,
and then I started to cry. A sadness began coming out of
me. It seemed as if I would drown in this sadness. I just
kept remembering the quote and sinking more and more
into the feeling. I didn't know or care why I was crying.
It felt as if those tears had been waiting all of my life
to come out. And now I was drowning in my own tears.
As the crying subsided, Les asked me what I was trying
to say. I wasn't aware of saying anything. I hesitated—it
seemed so difficult to say the words which were forming
on my lips. Each moment was more painful—and this
moment seemed excruciating. "In the destructive elements
immerse yourself . . ." I felt like I was breaking apart;
my stomach was contracted and felt as if it would rip
open. The only thing I was conscious of was the pain.
Then I was screaming and crying for mommy. I wanted
my mommy, and the pain of wanting her had finally
come out of the background. Each wave of pain brought
new memories and reactions. After a long and painful
immersion in pain of wanting mommy, I stopped crying.
I was drenched in sweat, and my arms and legs were limp
and numb. I was helpless. I was waiting, sweating; then
the crying began again—this time I felt abandoned and
heartbroken. There was only the pain. I was no longer
aware of any control—I knew where I was, but I was not

in control—I began squirming, writhing, crying, spitting up, and sweating—then a scene began to form in my mind. I was in the delivery room. Hot stinging liquid was being put into my eyes, my skin was stinging, and I hurt all over. I wasn't seeing the scene—I was reexperiencing it. Then I was in the nursery—I was crying and feeling desperate. Then a nurse picked me up and carried me to my mother. I was crying, feeling mother's warm body and eternally loving breast.

The session ended with a scene at my grandmother's house; she and Grandpa were looking at me. The pain had finally subsided and I was able to sit up and see Les. He looked completely different. I felt transformed. I could hardly believe the intensity of my experience.

I went back to the motel and slept. When I woke up it was early evening. I still hadn't eaten, but I wasn't hungry. I just waited. As I showered and dressed I became aware of new sensations and movements in my body. I was aware of my own movement. I was feeling very good until 9:30 or so. The awareness of motion and feelings was becoming more intense. I lay on the bed. I felt as if I had no legs, and an oversized head. Then my hip began to hurt. I asked myself: What is this pain? No intellectual answer. I just felt it was a very early experience—something to do with moving in the womb. Restricted and strained movement because of tight uterine muscles. All my thoughts were arising from sensations in my body. The sensations increased until I began to kinesthetically feel myself moving in the womb. I was pressing against a wall of muscle. I began to have a choking feeling and I started to panic—a thought came: I am not going to get out. I felt hopeless. I was suffocating while waiting to be born. I realized that I had to either have a Primal or stop the feelings. I was too afraid to call Les or to have a Primal by myself, so I sat up and wrote my experiences down. Finally early the next morning I was able to sleep.

TUESDAY

This morning I had four dreams that I remembered. Then I wrote in my journal, "I feel like the captain (in one dream a washed-out and defeated symbol). I am afraid of today's session. I feel tight in my chest, stomach, back, and legs. I am nauseated in my throat. I have no appetite. My insides feel dead. I feel like a dead baby. Stillborn. Not born. I should have called Les, but I am afraid of making any real demands. If I am still and quiet I won't hurt. If I cry and want I hurt more. My stomach hurts. I feel lost."

I was so apprehensive that I left the motel an hour before the session and waited outside. I was terror-stricken by the big speeding cars, the hurrying big businessmen, and the tall cold buildings. Finally it was ten o'clock.

SESSION TWO

I lay down and Les asked, "How do you feel?" "Little." I went with the feeling of being little. I was sweating and struggling for my life. I was submerged by feelings. I was in the womb, and each time I pressed against the walls there were powerful contractions. But before anything more happened the slide picture-like experience changed —now I was crying from the burning in my eyes and the stinging from my butt. I was crying from the pain of being handled. Then another switch and I felt diffuse then searing pain in my penis. I cried and cried—long, loud cries. Each sequence was anywhere from five to ten minutes long. The overall feeling was I had just been born and I was hurting. Then I began choking on phlegm from my nose, throat, and lungs. I was spitting up and screaming, when a nurse put me into an incubator. Hopeless waiting and I felt as if I was dying. Finally mother, and I sucked and choked and screamed.

I surfaced from those Primals feeling confused by the overwhelming, random, and vivid experiences. Nothing made sense. I felt weak and overthrown by my anarchical Primals. I was willing to feel pain, but I wanted it on my neurotic and orderly terms. I began talking to Les, and then he put me back into the chaos. This time I went into fetal positions. I began squirming. Then a ripple-like movement would come over me as I pressed against my mother's muscles. Periodically I would be convulsed by powerful uterine contractions which moved me slowly forward. This continued for what seemed like hours, and then three or four powerful contractions and I was out and exposed. I was there in black dizziness, adjusting to the nonwomb reality. Finally an instinctual and life-grasping scream came ringing out of me. I was crying from the pain of being born and the instinct to live. I felt completely vulnerable and unable to do anything about the pain of my new world.

Then experiences of going back and forth from the nursery to my mommy. Finally I was completely worn out. All I could do was lie on the floor and feel alive. Les and I talked for a while, but I felt unable to make sense of what was happening. I was falling apart and didn't care; in fact, I felt relieved.

During the next six weeks I reentered that Primal pool again and again. I began to know it as a birth pool. I had Primals about later experiences, but they would often only lead up to the birth pool. In the Primals that followed the first two days, a new logic was to emerge. The logic of pain. During the first two days I was overwhelmed by my feelings and thus was able to become open so that I would finally be able to feel completely the most critical Primal which was still lurking in the dimensionless pool of pain.

The birth Primals that followed the first two days were more specific and gave me more and more insights into my life. In what follows I have written only the highlights of those Primals.

ANOTHER SESSION

I lay down. I was feeling hopeless. Les got me to descend into that feeling. The memory came of lying in a crib and waiting to be brought to mommy—finally the physiological realization that mother wasn't receiving me. She was drawing away as I sucked. My reality was being taken away from me. I cried and cried.

ANOTHER SESSION

I was sitting on the floor suffering from pain across my shoulders and down my spine. Les helped me feel it.

Then the pain became movement and I was slowly rolling backward. I was again in the womb. This time the movement was infinitely slow. The movement put pressure on my spine because of the weight of my head and the difficulty of the motion. I was crying from the prenatal pain which had been felt but couldn't be fully experienced if I was to survive.

After each session I felt better, but I still had a general uneasiness. I felt paranoid at times and was still waiting for something more to happen. At the end of my second week of therapy Les sent me to visit my parents. That night I had a nightmare from which I awoke sweating and cold. I dreamed I was climbing a mountain but could never get to the top. I climbed and fell. I went to group the next morning. At first I was crying; no images or memories. I stopped and sat up. As I looked around the room I became very afraid and paranoid. Some intangible feeling was trying to come up and I was fighting it. I told Les of my fear, and he eased me into the craziness. I started to have a fit. I was sweating and terrified. I was being inundated by a feeling that was unbearable. I blindly reached out for help. Art took my hand, and then the feeling "endlessly" washed over me. The fit and screaming intensified—then stopped as an image came of me lying in an isolette.[1] The image was followed by feelings which were coming from inside of me and not overwhelming me. I was contracting and writhing from pain in the heart area of my chest. Wracking pain. I was dying. My heart was breaking. I kept crying and babbling until I sensed a body near me. A total body reaction to another body. I crawled, dragged, pulled myself under this body's legs. Once I was under the protecting, loving legs, I cried and cried. For the first time in my life I was safe. I wasn't going to die. I had survived.

[1] In recent talks with my mother I discovered the exact amount of waiting I had to endure as an infant. I was born at 2:45 in the afternoon and wasn't taken to her until 6:00 the next morning. Fifteen hours of waiting in a perfectly pure isolette. The most painful of all my Primals involved that waiting.

Two weeks later the pain came again. As before, it was preceded by the craziness, but when I finally felt it, the pain was duller but still very intense.

I was finally beginning to surface from the ocean of pain that had engulfed me. I reported afterward to Les a feeling of finally being on the beach. I was born and was going to live.

MY COMMENTARY

The crucial nature of the birth Primal is a result of the vulnerability of the defenseless infant organism. The prenatal, birth, and postbirth pains are not the cause of the neurosis—they are, however, such physiologically traumatic events that the infant develops a neuotic dynamic in order to maintain its existence. In this early pain-arresting reaction, the foundation for the neurosis is laid. The infant, in an all-or-nothing paradigm, must split itself off from the incoming pain, if it is to survive. This pain reduction permits the organism to go on. Thus the beginning of neurotic behavior.

DELIVERY ROOMS AND OTHER DENS OF INIQUITY

Imagine a critically sensitive organism in the relative dark and sensory isolation of the womb struggling to be born into plastic-wrapped hands or the icy grip of forceps. Once freed from its mother it is "treated" for birth and then saved from its own mother.

The infant, weak from its birth struggle and postbirth treatments, is taken to crib, isolette, or incubator and away from its only source of consolation and identity—mother. Mother, who is evolutionarily able to immediately provide consolation and identity through the heat of her body, is taboo. Identity and need are placed on a neurotic schedule made up by some expertly neurotic doctor.

There is evidence from infant mortality rates and emotional stability of newborns to indicate that our delivery rooms have institutionalized neurotic behavior. I believe it has become clear that if we intend to evolve and survive as a species we must at least discontinue socially accepted practices which are harmful to the full life of the infant—even if that act is sanctioned by the powerful and knowing "daddies" of the medical profession.

We will foster neurotic behavior as long as neurotic men and women create babies to get the love they never had, and doctors and nurses keep the hospitals on par with Renaissance churches, and baby bottles replace breasts, and drugs replace the pain and ecstasy of natural childbirth.

It is clear what must be done in preventive psychology, but as a therapist I am concerned with curing the already sick adult. The only problem in seeking a cure is my own illness. A neurotic, whether he is a psychologist or a plumber, thinks neurotically. Neurotic thinking is limited computer-like thinking which restricts us from feeling our knowledge. And only with feeling-knowledge can real change come about. This is clear with regards to the birth Primal.

Decades before Janov witnessed and finally felt the reality of the birth Primal, other psychologists were witnessing it.

> For this purpose they took him to the bedside of a female hysteric whose attacks were an unmistakable imitation of the birth process.[2]

> Hence the real transference-libido which we have to solve analytically in both sexes is the mother-libido, as it existed in the pre-natal physiological connections between the mother and child.[3]

> In attempting to reconstruct for the first time from analytic experiences the all too apparent [phenomenon] of a purely physical birth trauma with its prodigious physical consequences for the whole development of mankind, we are led to recognize the ultimate biologic basis of the psychical.[4]

[2] Sigmund Freud, *The Complete Introductory Lectures on Psychoanalysis*, tr. by James Strachey (New York: Norton, 1966), p. 303.

[3] Otto Rank, *The Trauma of Birth* (New York: Harcourt, 1924).

[4] *Ibid.*

Kelsy (1953) investigated fantasies of birth and prenatal experience and concluded that the fantasies represented actual events which had been repressed.[5]

But like Janov in his early work, they couldn't fully believe the reality or implications of what they were witnessing. Those who believed were still unable to do anything more than conceptualize and fit the experience into some theoretical niche. They were caught by their own inability to feel. If any one of them would have fully felt the experiences he witnessed, he would have discovered something akin to Primal Therapy. But to the "established neurotic" feeling is dangerous, since it brings him close to his own unfelt pain.

It is this lack of feeling which is the root of the failures of other therapies. Other therapists and therapies fail because when the therapist witnesses an event (Primal) in therapy which goes beyond his emotional tolerance, he stops the patient from "acting out," or from being "hysterical"—which is implicitly admitting that his theory and feeling capability cannot tolerate such an intensely emotional event. Thus therapists deny the experience of the patient in favor of their safe and mystified theories about what is real.

As a therapist and patient I am absolutely sure that the only theory I can believe is that which the patient creates from experiencing his own Primal Pain. Only as each patient unravels his mystery does his theory and cure come about.

A therapist who has not felt his own Primals will try to understand and analyze Primal experiences in a linearly logical way. But Primal experiences are not linear; they are spatially logical, which is to say, the patient is experiencing once again total organismic perception and memory which is his infant heritage.[6]

Thus between patient and therapist there is a dimensional gap—two-dimensional computer logic versus multidimensional feeling logic.

[5] Jesse Gordon, *Handbook of Clinical and Experimental Hypnosis* (New York: Macmillan, 1967), p. 222.
[6] This is akin to Freud's "polymorphously perverse." The polymorphous is the infants' and the perverse is Freud's.

No one can bridge this gap without first experiencing his own Primal Pain. For the Primal does not change your behavior; *it transforms you into yourself*.

R. D. Laing, in writing of the schizophrenic experience, describes this transformation.

> I have seen the Bird of Paradise, she has spread herself before me, and I shall never be the same again.
> There is nothing to be afraid of. Nothing.
> Exactly.[7]

In writing I have tried to render comprehensible some of the things I feel. I know I cannot tell you my experience because it is mine. I have found that I am the Bird of Paradise. Not your Bird of Paradise, but mine. I am my heaven and god and hell. I am molded by the very dynamics of evolution, but it is that fully felt pain which is transforming me into one—I AM.

As a psychologist I have got off the merry-go-round of understanding, and found the world of feeling. Finally I can be exactly who I am.

WHAT AM I TRYING TO TELL YOU?

> If I could turn you on, if I could drive you out of your wretched mind, if I could tell you I would let you know.[8]

Mary

I was at home late at night and felt very irritable and agitated. My body was unable to stay in any comfortable position. I again began to tremble much as I had done in the previous birth Primals. I had no control over my bodily movements. My hands, face, arms, legs, and torso involuntarily moved. I could feel sort of a "beep" in my head, and I waited quietly and my body responded to this sensation. It was as though my brain was sending signals down to the rest of my body. I knew that I was experiencing my first movements of life and was beginning to spurt out from a central point in my body and

[7] R. D. Laing, *The Politics of Experience* (New York: Ballantine, 1967), p. 190.
[8] *Ibid.*, p. 191.

radiate slowly in all directions, carrying with it a warming effect. The movements were in very slow motion, and I felt I was performing a water ballet. At the outset, movements occurred in my upper torso in rhythmic pattern. Then my tongue was hanging out of my mouth and started to quiver; gradually it drew itself in and out. From this, I spontaneously began to suck.

The "signals" were now radiating more strongly down my spine and moving into my legs. After much rhythmic movement, body contractions began and my body stretched itself out. Slowly I began to move downward in convulsive waves into the birth canal. I suddenly became terrified, and I was aware that something was being done to me from outside of the womb. My body was no longer involved in free, spontaneous movements. I was getting pulled from the outside—pounded and beaten.[9] I wasn't ready for what was happening. I was also aware that the something [placenta] was wrapped around my feet and I couldn't move them freely. The violent shaking began and I was quivering all over my body. The "beating" on the outside continued. I wanted to cry out for help, but couldn't. At this point, my hand became caught over my nose and I couldn't breathe freely.[10] I couldn't get my hand free from this position for a considerable time. My whole body vibrated with fear. No wonder I didn't want to be born. No wonder it took me so long to complete my birth Primals [the actual process took almost thirty hours, according to those present]. This relates to previous Primals that I have had relating to my legs and the inability to move them freely.

My body was literally "beaten" before I was born in their attempts to get me into proper birth position. I often wondered why I did not feel the actual intensity of the physical beatings I received from my mother as a child. Now I have the answer. It was too much for me to

[9] External manipulations performed by the physician to rotate the baby into the proper position for birth.

[10] The hand in this position would cause no difficulty in actual birth, as oxygen reaches the system via the umbilical cord. However, this caused a problem in reliving the experience.

endure during birth, and so I stopped feeling the beatings even then.

The portion that follows are excerpts from the actual recording that was taped immediately after my birth Primal [spoken with deep sobbing and weeping as insights were made]: ". . . There wasn't anybody to help me. Nobody—nobody. And nobody to see . . . nobody to see that I was in danger and that they were hurting me. They were imposing all their might upon me. Then my neck was being forced from side to side and the vibrations were setting off my whole body. Someone had me by the head and was trying to pull me and force me out.[11] [Forceps] . . . wriggling me and pulling me back and forth. When the placenta was around my legs and I couldn't move and I was being destroyed and couldn't call for help. No one could hear and no one could see . . . these were Primal Scenes for me. . . .

". . . When I was in the birth canal, I just needed gentle, gentle help . . . but no one was there to give that to me. It is a wonder that I survived. . . . I was hurting so much and I was so scared. . . . I just had to turn off and shut down. . . . I had no place to go. My mother could have been a real martyr if I died. She always has tried to play martyr all her life . . . then everyone could have said how she must have suffered . . . she suffered so much that she even lost her baby . . . no wonder she hated me . . . I survived and didn't let her have all the glory . . . that is why you were always jealous of me, Mommy. . . . That is why I always threatened you . . . you really wanted to keep me stupid so that I wouldn't know that you hated me so much. . . . You never wanted me . . . never, never . . . I want me . . . I want me . . . Mommy, Mommy . . . if you don't want me . . . and no one else wanted me . . . I want me now . . . me . . . me . . . I could only do what they told me to do . . . love me . . . please love me . . . me . . . me . . . me. I know now that an infant is all body . . . I am all body.

". . . All my life I have been running trying to find

---

[11] Delivery was almost complete.

someone that would see how much I needed and how much I hurt.

". . . I know that when my Primals unfold, they follow a consistent pattern. If they could be plotted, they would unfold in a natural sequence and natural order, but unique to me as a human being . . . my own individual way. I can see that consistency as they all link up together. The Primal scenes are basic because they are the basis for my connections. I also understand something about love . . . it is just letting be . . . I just am . . . it isn't being little, or big, or smart, or stupid, or anything. . . . Just is, that's all. I just am. It was safer for Mommy to keep me a little girl. She never wanted me to grow up, and she held me back from the start with her body. She had to keep me stupid from finding out that she really hated me and didn't want me. If she could keep me from growing up, the better chance she had of keeping this knowledge from me. I had to be dependent upon her for all the answers . . . that way she was safe. I had to be her favorite child so she could control me . . . and keeping me from finding out how things really were. . . .

"I know that what I experienced through my birth Primal was the beginning of my body physically shutting down. It couldn't absorb the pain that I felt. Since then my body has literally come alive in so many ways. I was taking four milligrams of thyroid medication daily before beginning therapy. I have not taken any since my first day and have a normal PBI. My normal temperature has dropped . . . how much I don't know but I recently had an infectious virus, my body knew the symptoms of high fever, yet the doctor recorded my temperature at 97.2. He couldn't understand the discrepancy. Also the skin over my entire body has begun to secrete its own lubrication. The dryness which was rapidly getting worse has reversed itself, and my skin has taken on a real glow. I really am just beginning to be alive for the first time in my life."

ANALYSIS

We see in these Primals the subtle interweaving of birth traumas and later behavior. They are not so much cause and effect as integral wholes, interrelated organismically. Getting stuck in the uterus became part of being "dumb" later on for her. That is, the uterine experience plus a need on the part of her mother to make her dumb in many thousands of ways covering many years of relationships combined to produce "dumb" unknowing, unaware behavior. Reliving the birth experience unraveled much of the later experiences with her mother for her. Her mother's need to keep her dumb later in life was just an extension of not allowing her to go her own way at birth. Thus the Primal birth experience of being stuck may be felt as a total helplessness rather than a "dumbness." Feeling "helpless" is an "interpretation" of experience. That interpretation comes with the use of language and the development of conceptual abilities. But the *feeling* of helplessness, of being powerless to shut off pain, begins with the birth experience in some individuals. That feeling is unconscious and unrecognized, but because it exists and was derived from a "life" experience, it drives behavior so that the person may act out being helpless later on in life (that is, feel helpless against a situation in which he has no power and act helplessly).

2. ON EPILEPSY

Introduction

There are different kinds of epilepsy with a variety of causes. The following section was written by a man who suffered from both grand mal and petit mal seizures before his therapy. He had been on Dilantin or Philantin, drugs used to control seizures, for years. What seems evident is that he was effectively "cured" of his epilepsy within a few weeks. What does that mean? Simply that he understands that his epileptic seizures are repressed Primals; that he can predict when his seizure/Primal is coming on and control it by feeling those painful feelings underlying it. He may go on having Primals for years, but he will not go on having seizures.

This man went off medication before therapy and rarely has had the need for any since. The one time he had a seizure while in treatment was when he was unable to come to group in the first few weeks of therapy, had an argument with his mother, and had no place to go and feel his Pain. The result: a seizure. Why did he have seizures instead of ulcers? It would seem that his prototypic trauma was the assault on his head during birth, as he so well describes. Another person continuously starved on a scheduled feeding regimen in infancy might later develop ulcers in response to tension. The overload of tension went to his head, evidently, because it was the first and most salient unresolved trauma of his life. What is becoming clear is that we can overload the brain by putting into it more than can be integrated and produce symptoms such as epilepsy, in much the same way that we can overload parts of the stomach with a hypersecretion of hydrochloric acid and produce ulcers.

One function of drugs such as Dilantin is to slow down the transmission of nerve activity through its effect on the sodium content of the nerve cell. This acts to stop the spread of nervous discharge from the site of the seizure area. In this way, random massive discharge of brain cells (a seizure) is prevented. What Dilantin does, evidently, is stabilize the threshold against hyper-excitability caused by excessive stimulation. The nerve cells become less responsive to repeated (Primal) stimulation. Dilantin does not make that Primal stimulation disappear, however. It suppresses it in the same way that other drugs may suppress the hypersecretion of hydrochloric acid and prevent an ulcer attack.

Primal Pains *are* repeated stimulations to the system. We see this on a simple level when we cannot sleep because of the pain of a toothache. The pain activates. It may also cause continuous constriction of the blood supply to the heart so that the person continuously must take vessel-dilating agents. Drugs, no matter how potent, do not *cure* any of those ailments; they suppress activation. The aim of Primal Therapy is to *remove* that activation permanently. If this is not done, then the pressure of a suppressed seizure may funnel itself into an allergy attack or a heart attack. We can see how medicine, by and large, has become basically a symptom-suppressing science rather than a curative one. And medicine has been preoccupied with the symptom exchange; changing one symptom for another. That is why as soon as one symptom is cleared up through drugs, a patient often develops something else; the tension is seeking another avenue of discharge.

If one could see the man whose story follows in a Primal, holding his head from the tremendous ascending pressure of Pain, writhing and thrashing on the floor for an hour or more, one could quickly understand how that pressure, when blocked, could become a seizure. Primals can look like seizures. Fortunately, they are not; they are the specific antidotes for seizures.

Simon

I am a twenty-four-year-old graduate student majoring in experimental psychology at the University of California, Irvine. Until I read *The Primal Scream*, I had absolutely no interest in therapy and anything associated with clinical psychology. Even though I was afflicted with a multitude of psychosomatic symptoms (hay fever, asthma, chronic headaches, hemorrhoids, and petit mal epilepsy), the thought of psychotherapy never occurred to me because I attributed all these symptoms to the pressures of graduate school, work, and trying to raise a family. After I read the introduction I was convinced that this was no run-of-the-mill psychology book. By the time I finished the book, I knew that it not only contained the answers to raising a family properly, but it also had the potential to change my life.

However, my biases toward therapy were not easily eradicated. It wasn't until a friend of mine who had gone through the first three weeks of therapy introduced me to Art Janov that I began to think seriously about Primal Therapy. By the time I met Dr. Janov, my wife had read the book, been affected so much by it that she began to have a nervous breakdown, and consequently signed up for therapy.

Shortly after I signed up, my wife was suddenly and unexpectedly called to start therapy within a week. We were both surprised and very happy, and I was sure that I too would start within a short while. However, I was soon to learn that no immediate plans had been made for my starting date.

During my wife's first week in therapy, I also learned that I was not the strong, independent person I had imagined myself to be. I was, in fact, very dependent on my wife, and trying to take care of myself and our three-year-old daughter made me realize that I could barely live without her. The "clincher" to the problems I encountered during that week was the news from Mrs. Janov that I probably would not be able to start therapy for another two months. An index of my illness that week was the recurrence (in full strength) of three of my symptoms—extreme hay fever and asthma and two petit mal seizures, both of which happened at night while I was asleep.

By the time her second week started, I was just sitting at home feeling absolutely miserable and crying more than I had ever cried in my entire life. It was so bad on that Tuesday morning that I called Art Janov and told him what was happening to me. He listened very patiently and told me to call back in two days, at which time he would be able to give me a starting time. This alone helped to alleviate the pressure for a little while, and I felt at ease for the first time in one and a half weeks. About an hour later the phone rang, and very much to my surprise, I heard my wife asking me how I was and could I pack my things and be at the Institute [the Primal Institute] in an hour? When I finally realized (and believed) what she was saying, I blurted out a "yes," packed some clothes, gathered up my daughter and her clothes, and was on my way to Los Angeles.

The only thing I can say about that 50-mile drive is that I'm damn lucky I didn't kill myself before I started therapy! I started to cry while I was on the freeway, and I felt as if I was losing complete control of my body. My head would jerk spasmodically and I was in a daze most of the time. I'm convinced that the only reason I found my way to the Institute was because I had been there several times before.

When I finally arrived there, my head (where pressure

had been building ever since I left our home) felt as if it were about to explode. It was all I could do to keep from screaming. The feeling inside my head was one of billions of neurons firing randomly and rapidly, completely out of control; there was literally an electrical storm brooding inside my head. Just to move it back and forth was agony; shaking it made me feel as if my brain were banging against the side of the skull and then chafing on the bone.

The only significant thing I recall about walking into the building was that I was told the very friend who had introduced me to Primal Therapy was going to be my therapist, and I felt rather good and secure about this.

The next thing I remember was starting my therapy; i.e., lying on the floor in the therapy room and beginning to unravel the mess I had made of myself. I won't describe the proceedings of each day of my therapy; instead I'll only concentrate on those Primals which had a direct bearing on the cure of my epilepsy.

On the very first day of my therapy I began what would prove to be the main Primal associated with my epilepsy —a birth Primal. I started this first session with many feelings about Daddy, and as I went on talking and yelling about him, the pain in my neck, shoulders, and head just became more intense. All the feelings I was having made the pressure become greater, and this finally made me start gagging and choking and rolling around the floor holding my neck and my head, both of which hurt immensely. My therapist told me to "let it out," but I couldn't because it was so intense. Then I remember feeling as if I were in a fetal position and suddenly my legs started pumping. I still didn't know what was happening, but as I pushed with my legs, my head started to hurt more and I moved it (involuntarily) closer to my chest. Suddenly I literally felt as if I had to get unstuck and I knew I had to push harder to do it. But the harder I pushed the more resistance I felt on my head. The overall experience was one of pushing as much as I could against an immovable object, and my head was absorbing *all* the resistance. I stopped (because of fatigue) a number of times, and the first time I stopped I told the therapist that I now knew that I'd had a headache all my life. Each time I stopped, I expressed some sort of pain, and when my therapist told me to feel it, I would just automatically start pushing again. I finally got too tired to continue, and I ended my first session feeling relieved, exhausted, and incomplete.

Two significant things happened on my second day in therapy: first, I was assigned to another therapist, and second, I continued the birth Primal I had started the day before. The most vivid thing about this section of my birth Primal was how fiercely and intensely I struggled to get out. I discovered that I was using my head as an "instrument" with which I would try to ram through the wall of muscle that was holding me. The more I rammed my head, the more it hurt and the more hopeless the whole struggle became. I finally got so tired and sore that I simply quit. As I was lying on the floor, I made a very meaningful connection for me. Whenever I slept alone (since as long as I can remember) I would always either have to rock my body back and forth or bang my head against the pillow in order to fall asleep. Now I realize that this was simply a reenactment of the birth struggle.

I started my fourth day of therapy with another section of the birth Primal. It started with the same problem that I left it with on the other two days—my head had that "stuck" feeling. However, this time I was begging Mommy to help me and I worked very hard—harder than ever before. Every time I rested, Bernie (my therapist) encouraged me to continue asking my mommy to help me. This usually got me right back into the Primal. When I finally got to the point where I couldn't take any more for the day, Bernie asked how my head felt. The best description that I could give was that it felt as if a warm towel were wrapped so tightly around my head that it was causing tremendous pressure pains. During the Primal, I actually felt as if the "towel" was like a band of muscles contracting on my head. It should be noted that this was the first day I really thought that what I was going through was actually a birth Primal. I had thought about this before on the other two days, but I was never really quite sure what all this meant.

The next day proved to be one of the best and most important days of my therapy, as far as the epilepsy is concerned. It was on this day that I finished my first birth Primal. I was feeling really shitty when I got to the Institute, and I had to work to keep myself from going down in the waiting room. When I was finally taken to my room, I was in such bad shape that I could barely get my shoes off. As soon as I was on the floor, Bernie simply said, "Don't lose that feeling, stay with it." I did just that and went right into the birth Primal. I was working furiously and frantically to get out like on the other days, but I really felt that I was hopelessly stuck. I labored until I couldn't do any more, then I yelled out for Mommy to help me. I tried to move again but couldn't, and the exact feeling I had was that I wanted to give up and pass out because it seemed that I just couldn't be born. I didn't really care anymore. But the pains on my head and body (especially the constriction around my head) were too great to ignore. Then, as I was lying there, I suddenly felt something working on my body. It felt like rhythmical contractions all over me, and my body simply moved with them. Later I told Bernie that it was as if I was completely wrapped up in a wet towel and someone was wringing it out over and over and, because I was inside, I was slowly being "gooshed" out. Then I felt the pressure on my head ease and I began to cry, but I was still being moved out and my body was still unable to do anything itself. I could feel Mommy working to get me out, and I knew I was crying from all the pain before I was even completely born. This fact was later verified.) Then, quite suddenly, the only sensation I was aware of was not being pushed anymore and just relaxing. My whole body went limp for a long time and I was really tired. When I started to come around long enough to talk to Bernie, I had to laugh because the feeling of being out and free was so fantastic!!!! He asked me how my head felt and I said it hurt. He told me to go with the hurt, but as I did, it went away. I described as best as I could to him what had happened. Then I made the connection that ever since my birth, I've been using my head as a battering ram. I have *absorbed* all pain with my head, and everything I've ever done being good at school, being a smart and clever boy, etc.) has focused around the use of my head. I guess you might say that my whole life had been a head trip. Bernie asked me if that meant anything to me in relation to my seizures, and I said that even though I couldn't make a mental connection right now, I'm sure that my seizures were just my head responding to too much pressure. I never let the rest of my body do any of the work; I simply stopped and bottled up all pain and feelings inside my head.

The next few days were spent in Primals that were not directly related to epilepsy and seizures. However, two things happened that are worth mentioning here. On one of the days, I was having some Primals about my uncle with whom I used to live. One particular Primal was concerned with wanting to both love and hate him. Thinking about this dichotomy gave me a "splitting" headache which turned into a real knotty feeling in my stomach. This physical feeling was identical to one I had when I had a Primal about Mommy and Daddy getting a divorce—I wanted both of them but I could have only one. The wanting of two things and getting only one in both cases related above gave me an unbearable headache which was, in the real sense of the word, a splitting headache. On another day, I felt the feeling of wanting to talk to my uncle but not being able to because he never listened. The exact feeling I had in my head during this Primal was one of a tug-of-war being waged inside my skull. This "tug-of-war" feeling was one I'd had for a long time whenever I wanted to do the impossible. Both of these feelings were very important to me because they revealed the nature of my major defense—absorbing everything in my head by thinking and intellectualizing.

The following Primal is related in its entirety because it is the first time ever that I have relived a seizure and subsequently recalled everything about it (including why it happened). Two important facts that should be mentioned first are that this was my first grand mal seizure (thus making me a true, diagnosed epileptic) and the slow, careful, and roundabout way I finally got to everything in this Primal.

I didn't feel much of anything when I started. I just lay there like a dead fish. Then Bernie said something like, "Go with the general feeling in your body," and I started to sink into something where I was breathing heavily and my whole body started to tingle. It was a frightening feeling because along with the tingling came a sort of numbness and I felt for an instant as if I were going to die. This feeling of death (or at least loss of consciousness) was so frightening and overwhelming that I shut it off involuntarily.

I told Bernie what happened, and he asked what that feeling was—had I ever had it before. I told him that I didn't know what it was, that I had begun to experience it the day before but only for a few seconds. He told me to just go into my body and feel whatever was there. I did, and the same feeling came again, except that it lasted a little longer this time.

This going in and out of this feeling happend two or three more times, but each time the feeling lasted a little longer and there was progressively more physical motion when the feeling came over me. Then Bernie and I talked for a little while about the physical things that came with the feeling. He also asked me what was happening outside of my daily therapy sessions. I said I wasn't doing too much, mostly just thinking, walking, shopping, eating, sleeping, and talking to Jane [his wife]. He asked if I talked to her last night and, if so, what about. I told him I was talking about my uncle and telling Jane about all the shit he laid on me when I was going to high school. As I was talking to Bernie, I suddenly began to breathe heavily—almost because I felt as if I couldn't breathe at all. I felt as if I were being choked. I told Bernie about it, and he asked what the feeling was.

I said that I felt as if my uncle always had us (my mother, brother, and myself) on strings—like puppets—and he was pulling them around us. Then the breathing became difficult again and I said that I felt as if there were a 50-pound weight on my chest. Bernie immediately had his hand on my chest and was pressing down heavily. I quickly became terrified and began to wail and yell. I think I even yelled out, "Get off, get off." This lasted for a few minutes, and when I stopped, I said that my uncle always had us under his thumb. That was where the feeling of pressure was from.

Then I began to remember a two-week period during one of my high school years when my uncle was laying the shit on me in more than usual quantities. I told Bernie that even though I didn't know why I said it was exactly two weeks, I just knew that it was a seemingly long period when everything I did was either too slow or wrong, or both.

While I was talking about this, I started to get sick to my stomach, and three or four times I had such real physical pain that I couldn't talk anymore because all I could do was feel a sickening and oppressive pain in my stomach and head. At one point the pain was so bad that I wanted to get away from it by telling Bernie about something that happened during the day, but he stopped me and made me continue with the feeling. Each time the pain subsided, I started to remember more about that two-week period, and each new memory or series of memories set off more pain. By telling Bernie a little about what was happening and by allowing myself to feel my body (go with it), I got into more and more stomach and head pain (it felt like some increasing pressure from within that was trying to get out) and also more memories. As far as I remember, this Primal ended with my yelling, "Let go, stop it." These phrases were repeated a number of times, and when I finished screaming, I was exhausted and just lay there for a while.

When I started talking, I was telling Bernie about the circumstances of my first seizure at home. I wasn't quite sure why I was talking about this just now, but he asked me some questions and I continued to answer. I told him about how I remembered coming to on the bathroom floor and seeing my mother, the doctor, and some neighbors; then looking out the window and seeing blue sky and being surprised that it was clear. I also remembered that I had missed my ride to school. Bernie asked me what the clear sky and ride had to do with these memories, and I said that I thought they were important, but I wasn't quite sure why.

Then I began to recall what happened after the doctor and my mom put me to bed. I slept for four or five hours, and when I woke up I saw the blue sky out my window again. It was then that I remembered that it had been raining for about a week and that day was the first clear day, and that's also why I was thinking about my ride to school because I sometimes took the bus when it wasn't raining.

Then I suddenly said that I had just remembered that after I woke up, my uncle came in to see me and find out how I was. He was very apologetic and hoped that it wasn't anything he said or did that caused all this to happen.

Now everything suddenly fell into place. It was like a gigantic puzzle falling from the sky, taking a long time to come down, but landing perfectly in place! The seizure had marked the end of a two-week period in the winter of my sophomore year in high school during which my uncle was on a continuous drinking binge and therefore was also giving me the worst possible shit for the longest period of time. It also suddenly occurred to me that it had been raining for the last week of therapy and today was the first sunny day (I'm sure that this helped to trigger my memories).

I told Bernie that it got to the point with my uncle where I just didn't want to listen to him anymore, didn't care about him, and, in fact, didn't care about anything. In short, I felt as if I just wanted to give up and die (like at birth). The pain was too great (in the head, because that's where I stopped it), and I just passed out—had a seizure.

I also realized that with all the shit I was getting from my uncle, I should *always* have been sick to my stomach, because that's what too much shit does. But not me— I used my head! Thus, my uncle was literally killing me and I didn't care anymore and just gave up and passed out (escaped from the pain).

Later I told Bernie that it was becoming very clear and obvious that I don't *need* to ever have seizures again because it now was simply a matter of asking myself whether I want to live or die; i.e., whether I want to have

Primals or seizures; because having seizures means to die. This realization made me feel very smart and very happy.

What was really interesting about this Primal and its connections is the way I got to the events surrounding my first seizure so slowly and carefully. As I look back on it, it is clear that the pain was so great that my body wouldn't let me do it any other way. It started with the gradual pecking away at what that two-week period was all about and feeling (for the first time) all that pain in my body and not just my head. Even this feeling of the pain was slow because there was so much of it.

Then, after it was all felt and I had recovered many of those memories, I began to talk about my first seizure without really knowing that that's what happened next anyway! Then came the gradual closing of the memory gap between my first seizure and those two weeks, until I realized that I was actually working with one sequence of events—not two separate events!

One other noteworthy Primal connection was made during my first three weeks of therapy. I had a number of Primals one day in which one theme was predominant —a trapped feeling. The trapped feeling eventually went back to my uncle's keeping me almost locked to the house (at least that was my feeling). This feeling of being trapped always produced a pressure sensation in my head, and after I finished this series of Primals I recalled that I stopped having seizures for about two years after my uncle died. The pressure feeling didn't come back until Jane was pregnant, and the seizures started again after our daughter was born. The fact that I didn't want to be a father at the time makes it "painfully" clear to me that the pressure of suddenly having a family was too much for me to handle. Therefore, the "overload switch" was again activated out of necessity.

The following Primals occurred after I had finished my three weeks of intensive therapy.

The first epilepsy-related Primal that I had in group was concerned only with the use of my head as a pressure-blocking device. Therefore, it is important because it clearly revealed to me the methods I employed (unconsciously) to cause seizures. I had returned to school for the first time since I began therapy, and spending the whole day in classes and at work on campus started a buildup of pain and pressure in my head that I felt in full force for the first time in my life. The entire Primal I had that evening was one of letting the pain flow from my head to my body so that I could avoid having a seizure (which I felt coming on). A very small part of this Primal was spent in asking my uncle and daddy to be strong enough so that I could lean on them for support. The insight that followed was that what I really wanted from them was to have them be the kind of people who could channel away some of my pain.

This next Primal was highly significant because it marked the first time I had a Primal about my mother and also because it was a direct result of my first and only seizure since I began therapy and stopped taking medication.

I had called my mother one morning to talk about some financial matters when she started to lecture me about the seriousness of the loan my parents had given us for our therapy. She sounded very much like my uncle, who always used to give me lengthy lectures about money and how to spend and save it, and this, in addition to the fact that I'd had a bad night (many unresolved feelings acted out in dreams), caused me to black out and have a seizure. As soon as I regained consciousness, Jane took me straight to the Institute for a private therapy session. The Primal I subsequently had was asking/begging Mommy to leave me alone and not be so overprotective.

It must be noted that this seizure was different from any other seizure I had ever had before therapy. First, I was aware that I was having a seizure a few seconds before it started (unfortunately it happened too quickly for me to stop it by turning it into a Primal immediately). Second, I didn't sleep for six or eight hours after the seizure—I only rested for about ten minutes. Third, the convulsions lasted a much shorter time and were far less severe than usual. Fourth, there was virtually no amnesia after I woke up. Formerly, it would take weeks and sometimes months to recall the events surrounding my seizures. Fifth, the minute I woke up, I felt unbelievably intense pain both in my body and especially in my head. Whenever I woke up from the sleep following a seizure before, I had a mild headache for about a week afterward. This time the intense pains I felt disappeared as I was having the Primal at the Institute, and they did not return afterward. All of this means that because I was starting to open up, my body would not allow me to store the unresolved pains of the seizure as it has been accustomed to do. This idea is clearly supported (for me, anyway) by the fact that I couldn't sleep and didn't have amnesia after the seizure.

Just recently I had another birth Primal, this time feeling much more intensely the struggle I had to go through to be born and the enormous pressures that my head came up against during that struggle. This birth Primal had by far more body pain and gagging and choking than the first one. To describe it in detail would simply be to repeat much of what has been described already, so I'll mention only the one new significant part of the Primal that occurred just before I was born.

I had got to the point where I gave up and just wanted to pass out because I felt as if I was doing all the work and couldn't do anymore, and then felt my mother begin to push me out. The extraordinary thing that happened this time is that as I felt myself being pushed out, I had a very strong urge to open my eyes and see "where I was going." When I tried to open them I found that I couldn't keep them open and all I was able to do was flash them rapidly. The reason I couldn't keep them open during the Primal (and probably birth) was that when I tried to look, two things happened: first, they stung unbearably even when I opened them for only a split second, and second, whenever they tried to open, all I could see (in the Primal) was a narrow but extremely bright spot of light. The combination of being able to see only a bright spot of light and flashing my eyes fairly rapidly as a result of trying to open them produced a feeling that was very much like that I'd had before when I saw a light flashing at the frequency that could induce a seizure. I am convinced that my sensitivity to light as an epileptic was a direct result of this eye-opening trauma at birth.

The latest Primal I've had about my epilepsy occurred at the end of one of the most hectic weeks I'd had since therapy started. However, the worst thing about this week was not that I was so busy but that I had a cold and this prevented me from going to group all week. The effect this had on my system was that I had a number of four- or five-second "daydreaming" periods all week long. They were not really dangerous—just annoying.

I started the group session by thinking about the condition I'd been in all week and what staying away from group was doing to me. I started to feel sorry for myself and couldn't understand why I had to be stuck with epilepsy. Art came over and I told him what I was thinking. He told me to go with whatever feelings I had about the seizures. Immediately the pressure/pain returned in full force and I felt as if I were going to have another seizure, but all I experienced was the pain of one. I realized then that I would have to relive and feel all the unfelt (and forgotten) pains of each seizure I've ever had. After all, the pain was stored—it just wasn't felt because of the sleeping I did and the amnesia I had.

When Art came back and asked what happened, I explained the whole series of events to him and I also said that I now realized that I had been two people living in one body—the "head" me and the "body" me. The only bridge that connected the two was my epilepsy—it kept my head from making my body do the impossible; i.e., it was the overload switch that kept my circuits from burning out and killing me.

These, to date, are the Primals I've had that were directly related to my epilepsy. I'm sure that without these particular Primals, I would still be having seizures like I did before. I think it's important to mention at this time that the day I started my therapy, I stopped taking my medication, and I haven't taken any since then.

There is simply no more need to take the medication because there is no more need to have seizures. If this sounds like an extremely simple statement, that's only because the solution to the problem of having seizures is that easy. Since I know now that a seizure is ony a repressed Primal coming to the surface too rapidly to be properly integrated and handled, all I need to do is have Primals. The week during which I couldn't go to group and, as a result, had pseudoseizures all week attests to that fact. A friend to whom I've described what I stated in this paper has offered the cirticism that I've become a "Primal addict." I couldn't agree more; after all, what's better— to be a "Primal addict" or a raging epileptic for the rest of my life? The only regret I have is that I can't turn the other four million epileptics in this country into Primal addicts!

In summary, then, my environment (from birth) forced me to adopt a life style that would allow me to protect myself from the repressive forces I encountered. I employed all the symptoms described in the opening paragraphs to defend myself daily, but when the pain became too great for even these defenses, my system simply reverted to the use of its first natural defense against pain —the desire to black out which frst occurred at birth. This defense was acted out in the form of epileptic seizures. It also wasn't until I had relived the birth trauma that I could stop having seizures. That is why I had a birth Primal so early in therapy. That is, the seizures were the Achilles' heel that had to be discovered so that I could open up.

This Achilles' heel theory has been verified for me personally by the fact that many of my Primals now (and all of my early Primals) started out with the physical feelings associated with the beginning of a seizure. Thus, the main defense (in my case, epilepsy) had to be punctured before I could open up by breaking down the rest of my defenses.

As I look back on how my body had always responded to pressure, I now see a continuum of defenses that it used to throw up. First, I would get a runny nose and hay fever attacks. If this wasn't enough to remove me from the painful situation, the asthma would begin to cut in. The last step prior to an actual seizure was a "splitting" headache. It's almost as if I was always giving myself a chance to remove myself from the causes of the symptoms a number of times before the last defense was actually employed; i.e., my system was sort of protecting itself in the best way that it could from the use of its most extreme (and dangerous) method of escape.

Something needs to be said about the migraine headaches. I referred to them earlier as "splitting" headaches because I experienced them during therapy when I had Primals about the following "splits": (a) to be born or not to be born (I gave up pushing when I felt I couldn't do anymore); (b) wanting both Mommy and Daddy when they were fighting and splitting up (couldn't have both); (c) wanting to both love and hate my uncle; and (d) at each of these three times and many other times when the overload of pain was too great, wanting to both live and die; this choice was acted out by having a seizure (thus to live means to have Primals and to die means to have seizures).

The epilepsy, of course, is not the only thing that has disappeared. All the symptoms I listed in the beginning either are gone or are going away. In addition, my life style has changed considerably, all as a result of discovering Me. As I find out who I really am, there is no more need to try so hard to be someone or something else. Thus, the self-induced pressures that were driving me before are slowly being removed along with the symptoms that came with the pressures.

3.   DOES CHILDBIRTH MEAN PAIN?

Introduction

The following chapter was written by Patti Nicholas, a parent and hospital consultant on natural childbirth. She instructs expecting parents on how to have a drug-free birth. The implications of what she has to say are important because she indicates that there is little reason for the tremondous pain during childbirth. Though there may be some simple pain resulting from the pressure of the fetus making its way out of the womb, it would appear that most of the pain can be accounted for by neurosis; more specifically, that the musculature of the neurotic woman (which includes the uterus) is continuously tense and tightened and lacks flexibility. The tension of the uterus, the tendency to clamp down instead of open up, is the main cause of pain in childbirth.

Thus, in normal women there would be no need for the drugs now used on so many women in labor. From what we have seen of birth Primals, these drugs do affect the fetus and provide a numbed entrance into the world. Far better to come into life alive, feeling and fully sensing.

Childbirth—Does It Have to Be Painful?

Childbirth is in accord with the natural rhythm of life and the universe. Menstruation and gestation follow the 280-day lunar cycle, menstruation usually being 28 days, and gestation 40 weeks. When a prominent, conservative physician (OB-GYN) was asked whether there were in fact more births during a full moon, he replied, "Let's just say that I hate to be on call during a full moon."

Lower animals have what is termed an instinctual birth. Each animal has its way of giving birth, and it is repeated in exactly the same manner throughout the years, regardless of environment. A dog living in Alaska with Eskimos would give birth the same way as a dog living with a suburban family in Los Angeles.

Human beings have what is termed cultural births. Women have approached pregnancy, labor, and delivery conditioned to expect certain experiences and to react in the traditions of the society and the culture in which they live. This has been going on since earliest times, perhaps since the brain became more complex. It is commonly believed that human beings can no longer respond on an instinctual level to childbirth. It is further held that as a result they can no longer have the "natural" or the easier labor and deliveries of the lower animals.

CHILDBIRTH PROCESS

Birth is the bridge between two different stages of life. It is the end of the gestation period inside the womb and the beginning of what should be the continuity of gestation (the newborn should not yet be thought of as something apart from his mother) outside the womb.

The baby is conceived in the oviduct, nutured in the

uterus. The uterus is a hollow, muscular sac that is very elastic and expands with the baby's growth. When certain stimuli occur, the uterus expels its contents with a series of contractions.

The uterus, like the bladder and rectum is a visceral organ. There are natural urges to perform. In a natural state the body would meet the demand before discomfort arose. If these natural urges become uncomfortable—when the bladder should be emptied or there is a strong desire to defecate—the body experiences visceral pains. It is an indication that the physiological balance is being strained.

When the oxygen level in the placenta drops, it causes the placenta to cease manufacturing progesterone. When the amount of this hormone diminishes, the muscles in the uterus respond by contractions.

The uterus is composed of three layers of muscles. Contraction of these muscles depends upon nerve supply. There are three sources of nervous impulse that send stimuli to the muscles. With harmony of muscle action the longitudinal muscle fibers contract and their action is expulsive. And in normal conditions, the circular muscle fibers are relaxed and flaccid, allowing dilatation of the outlet of the uterus and free passage for the baby.

The birth canal or vagina is approximately 4 inches of elastic muscle that should readily stretch to eight times its normal size. (The average woman's pelvic structure should easily accommodate the passage of an 11-pound 9-ounce baby.)

The uterus continues its rhythmic contractions, applying steady pressure and easing the stretching of the vagina by pushing forward and moving back slightly. When the baby begins to "crown" (enough of his head is out of the external outlet to set a crown upon), the pressure of his head cuts off the blood supply around the vaginal outlet, anesthetizing it and permitting the baby's presenting part to be born. Once the presenting part is born the rest of the body quickly follows.

There is no physiological function of the body which gives rise to pain in the normal course of health. The uterus is lined with "nociceptors" (pain receptors). The internal organs, especially the uterus, are not affected by external cold or heat. The abdominal wall has to be severely injured before it can be damaged. But it is well supplied, as is the uterus, with pain receptors which cause excessive tension or laceration of the tissues. The intestines and uterus can be burned, cauterized, handled and moved without any sensation of discomfort to the patient, but if either of these structures is stretched or torn, considerable pain and shock result. All nociceptors react to only one form of pain stimulation. It follows then that the only pain stimulus that the uterus can record is excessive tension or actual tearing of tissues. If nature did not intend childbirth to be accompanied by laceration and injury, those pain receivers are there to respond only to abnormal stimuli.

If the mental condition of the laboring woman disturbs the integrity of the contractions and increases their intensity, the thalamus in conjunction with the cortex immediately sets up protective measures. Now the sympathetic nervous system sets up a defense system of tension which increases muscular power. The branches which supply the circular muscle of the uterus are stimulated by this reaction and create a rigidity in the organ's outlet. This causes resistance to the longitudinal fibers. Now the muscle groups are in opposition, the longitudinal muscles struggling to dilate the cervix and the circular fibers restricting the outlet. (The circular fibers must necessarily restrict the outlet until the termination of the pregnancy.)

Persistent tension of the uterine muscles prevents relaxation between contractions. This deprives the uterus of venous blood, causing what is known as a white uterus (ischemic). So although there may be no anatomical obstruction, labor is inhibited by strong but ineffective contractions. Because of excessive intrauterine pressure and restricted oxygen supply, the baby is not able to survive the protracted labor and vaginal delivery.

Impairment of circulation is a cause of pain because blood flow is too small to dispose of metabolites (waste products of muscular action). A long labor, therefore, could be long because it is painful, not painful because it is long.

The chemical changes that occur when parturition is

disturbed seriously impair mother and child, altering labor and being responsible for hemorrhage, tissue injury, anoxemia, respiratory failure, and exhaustion in the newborn.

THE INFANT

The drop in oxygen that causes the hormone progesterone to drop in level also decreases the efficiency of the placenta as a lung for the child. The child's own system is alerted and the processees begin that will make the baby biologically independent.

The child's blood begins to use the arteries and veins between the heart and lungs. The digestive system, the lungs, the eliminative systems, the nervous systems, and the endocrine glandular system all prepare to function.

The contractions serve to stimulate the baby's skin. There is evidence that this is extremely important. It is suggested that without this stimulation the gastrointestinal genitourinary system and the respiratory system might not function well.

Animals lick the skin after birth to provide stimulation. Veterinarians know that without maternal licking, a newborn mammal will likely die because it is incapable of bowel and bladder elimination. The peripheral sensory nerves in the skin are stimulated. These nerves conduct impulses to the central nervous system and are shunted out to various organs of the body. When stimulation of the skin is inadequate, principal organs fail to act. This hypothesis has been evidenced by the work of Professor James A. Reyniers, who is in charge of the laboratories of bacteriology at the University of Notre Dame.

Thus, premature babies (who usually have short labors) or babies born of a caesarean operation receive less stimulation. These children, studies have found, do have more difficulty breathing and achieve sphincter and bladder control later and with greater difficulty.

In normal birth the chest of the baby is compressed as it passes through the birth canal. This induces considerable pressure within the chest cavity, heart circulatory system, lungs, and diaphragm. Furthermore, by its contractions the uterus squeezes blood from the placenta through the umbilical cord and into the baby. In the absence of prolonged contractions (caesarean), the baby does not receive as much blood. There is a failure to expel amniotic fluid from the baby's upper passages. Inadequate aeration of the respiratory tract occurs, as well as inadequate stimulation of the circulatory system.

The baby is propelled down the birth canal. The amniotic sac breaks and the child is exposed to air. Changes in pressure and temperature take place immediately. The diaphragm begins a bellows-like action which inflates the lungs with air, causing them to press upon each side of the heart.

I believe that if it were not good for the baby to be born via uterine contractions and through the birth canal, then nature would have devised a pouch or some other means for birth. Evidence shows that the activity of birth is beneficial to the well-being of that baby. Dr. Sandor Ferenczi says, "The more I observe, the more I realize that none of the developments and changes that life brings find the individual so well prepared as for birth." I think that it is important to an individual's physical and mental condition that he have a smooth birth. Births today are defined as medically or "method" normal. But by no means should we consider delayed labors (interference or malfunction of hormones?), prolonged labors, painful labors, ineffectual labors, or perhaps not even malpresentation (traverse or posterior position of baby) normal. It would appear that because a child's oxygen level is low his perception of pain is low. The newborn can be traumatized because the birth is abnormal. And today in our society most births can be put into that framework.

Freud contended that birth is the cause of an "anxiety condition" because of a life danger. He said that it produces a sense of helplessness and that the person develops a lifelong sense of dependence, a need to be loved. Otto Rank, in a series of books beginning in 1924 with *The Trauma of Birth*, saw birth as a rude interruption of blissfull uterine life. He believed that the individual spends the rest of his life trying to recover. There have been studies done on premature children and instrument-delivered children that clearly point out that they are disadvantaged.

And now there are the overwhelming birth Primals which prove in toto that trauma is most definitely caused at birth. Should this be? Should we accept the fact that it is the nature of birth to cause those conditions that would lead to the trauma?

I believe that birth is a physiologically normal and relatively painless process. When a society-conditioned woman is out of touch with her realities and the rhythm of her own body, her labor and delivery will be changed accordingly, presenting some or great trauma to herself and the newborn.

Babies should not be physically held back from being born until the doctor arrives (sometimes 45 minutes). If babies could be born normally, without pain, doctors would not be allowed to interfere no matter how persistent those doctors might become. Only because babies cannot be born this way do women need physicians to deliver them of their child. It is why they need drugs or the currently popular various methods of preparation (another pain-killer). Pain is undeniably present in today's childbirth. To say otherwise would be to misrepresent to the woman the work she must be prepared to deal with. But why?

A Case History

Brenda B. Age twenty. Married to minister. Home delivery.

Delivery began with rupture of waters 9 A.M., October 21. Contractions remained irregular throughout the day, although causing a great deal of discomfort. Contractions stopped while her mother and sister and father visited for two hours. Contractions resumed when they left.

The contractions were felt very strongly by Brenda. She was unable to contend with them with means other than total concentration on her labor coach's (husband's) instructions. He would have to do the breathing with her.

The cervix stuck at 8 centimeters and remained so for six to eight hours (the cervix is supposed to dilate from 7 to 10 centimeters in about fifteen minutes to one hour in a normal first labor).

Baby was born with a ridge on its head showing where

it was stuck in cervix. Waters showed meconium (child's first excreta, normally performed after birth), which doctors interpret as fetal distress. A midwife, asked the meaning of meconium in the waters, promptly replied, "The child is frightened."

The baby, born without drugs, what some would call a "natural delivery," was a month overdue (caused by inability of body to excrete proper hormones?) weighed 9 pounds, was fussy, crying, had incoordinate sucking reflex. Once he caught on, he still remained fussy and irritable. He demanded many feedings and did not seem able to get his needs met.

Postscript

After Patti Nicholas wrote the first article on childbirth and pain, we discussed her thoughts. Several weeks later, I received the following letter:

Dear Art,

When we first spoke about pain-diverting methods of prepared childbirth, you said, "Why divert women from the pain? Why not let them experience it?" Because my whole orientation as a childbirth teacher has been to "deal" with or avoid pain, I see now that at that time I could not permit myself to even consider the idea. A labor room full of screaming women has been something we've been trying to avoid. I have been diverting women from their pain (even though it possibly should not exist in normal women) rather than have them submit to the possible harmful effects of drugs.

But the more Primal ideas grow on me, the more it flashes on me that feeling feels marvelous—especially if one is in an environment where it is not only acceptable to scream but encouraged. The idea is we should really feel the wonderful experience of childbirth—pain and all. Maybe just by fully experiencing and expressing the sensations of childbirth, there would be a release of other tensions which create pain and produce backaches, headaches, etc.

I recall my only labor. Screaming during contractions

helped me. It made the pain feel good. Although between contractions (and not yet into Primal notions) I was so embarrassed and apologetic. I felt that I had lost control and was frightening other laboring women who would hear my screams. During it all I had to keep reassuring my doctor that it wasn't as bad as it sounded; as long as I screamed it was really fine. After the baby came out I had no feelingabout having been in such pain.

What if we did permit and encourage women to express their pain? If women knew up front that they could scream freely, many of the tensions and symptoms might be reduced in the entire labor process. What happens now is that nurses and doctors tell these women to be brave, act their age, etc.; they are upset because women are losing control. I think that the true expression of pain would help women *relax* (they wouldn't be aggravated by guilts and embarrassments) and have *less* pain in childbirth.

Women come to me usually because they are petrified of pain and they pay me for a method to alleviate it. It just never occurred to any of us that pain could be tolerated *if expressed*. That much of the "stiffening up" is not so much against the pain as its *expression*. I know we'll have a difficult time with doctors because they revert to the use of medication when they hear screaming. So we'll all need reeducation.

Sincerely,
Patti

Birth Trauma and Related Research

A conference on birth trauma was held in Puerto Rico in 1956. The proceedings of that conference, attended by the world's experts, was published under the title *Neurological and Psychological Deficits of Asphyxia Neonatorum.*[12] Selected research findings indicate that proper birth procedures are a matter of life and death, both from the point of view of medical management and in terms

[12] Edited by W. F. Windle, E. H. Hinman, and P. Bailey (Springfield, Ill.: Charles Thomas Co., 1958).

of having a mother-to-be as free from Primal Pain as possible.[13]

In 1938 a report was issued by two scientists who indicated that "the majority of cases of early neural damage could be ascribed to neonatal anoxia resulting from anesthetics and analgesics given to the mother during labor, and that lesser degrees of brain damage, too slight to come to the attention of the neurologist, could result in the same manner" (16). There is ample evidence that anesthetics cross the placenta and affect the fetus. Demoral given to the expectant mother depressed the blood oxygen. What happens then is that the newborn is oxygen-starved. When the starvation is severe enough, there can be brain hemorrhage and damage. One study found that "98% of infants born of non-drugged mothers breathed spontaneously [at birth] whereas only 65% of those born with mothers given the best drug combination did so" (16). In a review of 500 cases of cerebral palsy, it was found that heredity was an unlikely cause, and that neonatal anoxia (oxygen starvation) produced athetoid cerebral palsy.

Another report indicates that not only is there gross cerebral damage from improper birth, but that more subtle pathologies may result. "Behavior difficulties such as distractibility and hyperactivity result. . . . The correlation of abnormal labor is correlated with personality traits such as seclusiveness, egotism, over-affectionateness and emotionable instability" (21). Other traits found associated with abnormal labor were "variability of mood, hypermotility, impulsiveness, short attention span, bad memory and difficulty with arithmetic" (22).

One of the concomitants of anoxia is that the heartbeat is dangerously slowed. If the new baby is to survive, adjustments must be made instantly. One adjustment which has been suggested is to give the mother additional oxygen so that the fetus has a higher saturation to cope with the

[13] I shall not list the names of the research investigators, but indicate by parentheses the page on which the research may be found in the published proceedings. Those interested in further study may refer to the volume itself.

stress. A difficult labor means that the newborn is literally fighting for his life.

One of the factors in this fight is the alterations in hormone balance. "The evidence points to the conclusion that anoxia produces the typical stress response in the adrenal" (126). It also reduces "the I [iodine] uptake by the thyroid gland" (128). Histological studies of the thyroid gland "show alterations which are indicative of reduced activity" (128). It is the Primal contention that these radical alterations in hormone output become prototypic so that later stress induces the same response (say, of lowered thyroid output). As early stress mounts and the child becomes neurotic, the hormone alteration response becomes chronic. I use the term "response advisedly, since the glands and organs respond to stress like any other part of us.

Because hormone output does adjust properly on most occasions when oxygen is sufficient, we have been deluded into thinking that all was well. We have neglected the fact that we have set up an organ vulnerability—a target area which is later more responsive to stress.

A Baltimore study yielded the following results: "If you divide the whole Baltimore series, which comprised 10,00 mothers, into those who received drugs which cross the placenta and those which do not, there were differences in the fetal outcome. With drugs . . . there were delays in breathing and crying times which did not appear in patients who had drugs that do not cross the placenta" (238). What all those statistics mean is that a child cannot catch his breath and is in a desperate struggle to live.

The sensitivity of the newborn was pointed out in a study of caesarean babies. If the baby has his face touched during the birth process in low cervical operations the umbilical cord constricts. "This alteration in circulation makes blood difficult to obtain and oxygen values low" (242).

If we think about the staggering results of difficult labor, ranging from death to mental retardation, learning problems, hyperactivity, and severe hormonal deficiencies, we can see that the necessity to arrange proper birth is of paramount importance. In a myriad of ways many of us act out our birth Primals for the rest of our lives. We suffer from inexplicable tension. As one patient put it, "I never could sit still in class. I had the desperate feeling when I sat down that 'I had to get out.' Now after my birth Primal I know what I really had to get out of." If we can at least give ourselves the proper start in life, we will have more resources to cope with situations that later try to bend us. If we start out "bent," there isn't much hope.

BIBLIOGRAPHY

Montagu, Ashley. *Life Before Birth*. New York: New American Library, 1964.

Bookmiller, Mae M., and Bowen, George L. *Textbook of Obstetrics and Obstetric Nursing*. 4th ed., New York: W. B. Saunders, 1969.

Shabon, Irwin. *Awake and Aware: Participating in Childbirth Through Psychoprophylaxis*. New York: Delacorte, 1969.

Dick-Read, Grantly. *Childbirth Without Fear*. 2d rev. ed. New York: Harper, 1959.

Kitzinger, International Publication Service. New York: 1964.

IV. The Differences Between Physical and Psychophysical Therapies

1. INTRODUCTION

I have shown how reverberating Primal circuits affect our thinking and our visceral reactions. I have indicated that psychotherapy deals with those thinking processes which are secondary or derivative from Primal feelings while medicine treats the somatic, visceral reactions to those same repressed feelings. There is another form of therapy variously known as bioenergetics or orgone treatment. These are basically Reichian-oriented approaches, and they deal with the musculature. They are based on the belief that the body forms an armor around feelings and that the way to help a person become feeling is to attack the body armor. Thus, patients pound pillows, have their muscles pounded and kneaded, are forced to gag to ease throat tension, and so on. Primal Therapy has some times been equated with these physical therapies because of the physical action involved, as opposed to conventional psychotherapy. But the differences, I feel, are profound and should be clarified.

The essential difference between Reichian and Primal methods I see as the difference between an external-physical one (Reichian) and an internal-psychophysical one (Primal). The Primal view is that body armor—the tensing of the musculature—is the *result* of what has happened to us in life. The way to resolve that armor is to delve into those events, not to work backwards and try to release feelings by softening the physical armor. A patient pounds a pillow in Primal Therapy in the *context* of a very real anger about some remembered scene. A patient pounds a pillow in Reichian therapies at the direction of a therapist who is trying to loosen him up. These are two very different experiences. Pounding in Primal Therapy flows from inside out, from feelings. Pounding in the physical therapies tends to be contrived. The feeling releases the muscle tension in a permanent way, for muscle tension is part of the apparatus for repressing feelings.

In pre-Primal stages of therapy, some patients will pound a pillow and still be left with muscle tension because the reverberating memory circuit which produced that bit of tension has not been connected and resolved. What Reichian therapies try to do is release neurotic tension; Primal Therapy attempts to get at the source of the muscular tension. There are essentially two sources for this tension. First, there is the general muscle tension which comes from the Primal pool—the stiffening against the feelings. Second, there is a specific Primal feeling which can produce specific tension in certain muscle bundles. For example, one patient had a characteristic soreness in her shoulders and arms for years. During a Primal she felt the source—"I was always holding back from pounding my mother." Another patient had a Primal screaming: "Get off my back. Get off my back!" He had had backaches for years and never connected them to being weighted down with chores and responsibilities early in his life. The Primal came about when he was discussing how he always had to take care of his two younger brothers, and every time they got hurt he was blamed. He never felt the real feeling until therapy—that he shouldn't have been caring for anyone at the age of eleven. Still another patient felt the source of the pain in his neck he had had for most of his life. These pains usually turned into "tension headaches." That source was having his head violently rotated during a difficult birth. It was the prototypic response to later stress.

Reichian therapy would attempt to deal with the presenting tension. Primal Therapy understands that there are specific memory circuits at work innervating the muscles to produce tension; that excess muscle tension, more than we need to move ourselves around, *is* neurotic and therefore must be Primally derived. It is true that we use our bodies to lock in feelings. And it is true that we can occasionally get to those early feelings by unlocking the body armor. But concentrating on the body, I submit, is neither systematic nor predictive (as we shall see from the chapters written by patients who have had years of

Reichian treatment). Working on the body is again trying to solve problems from the outside in, when the problems exist inside. One reason that both psychotherapy and body therapy try to solve problems externally is that therapists think they can solve someone else's problems, that people need an "expert" to perform magic and other incantations on them, when all they need is themselves and to experience that self. If problems cannot be solved from the outside, then experts are not needed and that eliminates the need for an elitist class which has special knowledge about others.

Body approaches are the parallel to the Behavioristic or Conditioning therapies. Both strike me as mechanistic. Both try to change behavior mechanically, although the body approaches are certainly more interested in feelings than the Behaviorists. Both neglect sources as primary targets. For example, take a child who is constantly told to "shut up." When he is never allowed to sass, then he must hold his feelings in. He must hold them in because they exist and need to come out. No matter what he tells himself, no matter how accommodating he becomes around his parents, if they produce conditions which frustrate the child and make him angry, those feelings exist inside. Because they are a force he must enlist the aid of his body to stifle them, so he will automatically constrict his throat to choke off the feelings "at the pass," or he will bind them by tightening his stomach muscles. Having this person gag to loosen his throat has no permanent effect in the same way that punching his stomach muscles only temporarily lets sme feelings out. This person really needs to explore those early scenes where his parents shushed him, and he needs to be allowed to scream at them in the therapy office. His muscles will let go to the extent that he can tolerate the ascending Pain.. They will close down again and become tight in order to hold back more Pain than can be integrated. The point is that muscle tension is *protective* and should not be interfered with in any mechanical way.

An extension of bioenergetics is a technique called Rolfing (after its innovator, Ida Rolfe). This is essentially a body realignment approach in which posture is changed by vigorous manipulation of muscle bundles. The central aim of Rolfing is to soften the body's musculature so that bound energy is freed, producing a fluid body state. It is usually a very painful process. Sometimes, during Rolfing, Primal feelings erupt. The aim is usually not to elicit those feelings, but it is obvious that as muscles that bind feelings are relaxed, those feelings will come up. I liken Rolfing to the LSD experience; we might say that Rolfing is like an acid trip of the body. That is, it is a massive assault on the physical armor much as LSD bombards the mental defenses. The problem is that both are too much too soon. This does not mean that loosening body defenses is not helpful. I think it is—when done in a Primal context where the aim is at early neural circuits and not simply to achieve muscle relaxation as an end in itself. I am sure that certain bodily manipulations could be helpful in certain Primal patients at the proper time. Perhaps a patient is ready to undergo certain early experiences but his body is so tied up that it cannot cooperate. I am thinking of the barrel-chested man, for example, whose feelings are literally encased. Working with the fascia of the chest, shoulders and neck might well facilitate getting at feelings. Knowing the location of key muscle systems is as important for the Primal Therapist as understanding mental defense mechanisms. But the aim in dealing with mental (or physical) mechanisms is not an end in itself—but a means to get below into Primal feelings.

A Primal therapist would work at certain muscle bundles when a patient was ready for such an experience. It would be *in context* and not done in a haphazard manner. When not done in context, any physical manipulations are random—like free association of the body. There is no way to know in these approaches what a hunched or stooped shoulder means. It could mean, for example: "I'm afraid of showing my breasts because daddy doesn't like girls," or, "I don't want to show my chest and be sexual," or any number of things. The stooped shoulder, then, is part of a historic defense system and will be changed when a person relives the myriad of experiences associated with that central feeling. Now, one could manipulate the fascia of the shoulders and chest and produce erect posture, but the questions are will it hold up and, more important, what has happened to the reasons for that poor posture. They are still there. Those memory circuits still produce their load of tension, now rerouted, but still in the system somewhere. We have found that when the key Primal feelings are relived, posture straightens itself out. In short, posture is a memory, too—it is the reciprocal of the neural circuit. It is part of the *overall* defense system, not an entity unto itself.

I believe that any approach such as Rolfing which is so painful must be anti-natural. What is natural for neurotics is to be defended. Muscles are responding to a stored history of Pain. Releasing that *history* is what cures; not releasing the *results* of that history.

There is no doubt that tension relief can occur in physical therapies ranging from Rolfing to dance therapy. And when these physical therapies result in ascending Primal feelings, there may well be changes in the EEG. But we must keep in mind that moving *as an adult*, say, in dance class, is not the same as moving *as a baby*—as that baby who was not allowed to move freely. Moving and thrashing while reliving a crib scene where one was bound tightly with blankets are a *resolving* experience, while throwing the body around in dance therapy is an ameliorating one.

The Primal Pool of Pain is like a running spring, always in search of new outlets. Take away the postural defense and perhaps one's ulcers may become worse. Or somewhere else the system must take up the slack. It is very much like some kinds of psychotherapy in which the patient is encouraged to say all the forbidden words he could never say—to "shake out" his mind, so to speak. But the sexual inhibitions laid down early in life will still remain. Thus, one can speak or move freely and yet be doing something very mechanical, going through the motions of freedom without its essence.

Body therapy is essentially a confrontation approach. An expert confronts the physical front. In encounter therapy, he encounters the personal-social front and tries to redirect it. But one can confront only himself. One's destiny must always be shaped from within if man is to grow naturally. Neurosis occurs precisely because one's destiny has been shaped from outside. Neurosis means being molded, body and mind, into an unnatural state by others. It does not help to be remolded into another shape decided upon by someone else. One must have his own destiny handed back to him. Man needs only to be his natural self; there is no state beyond that.

The following sections, written by Primal patients who had years of Reichian therapy, illustrate some of the differences I have discussed.

2. A PERSONAL COMPARISON OF PRIMAL AND ORGONE THERAPIES

Roger

The therapy of emotional disorders which is most similar to Primal Therapy is orgone therapy, which was developed by Wilhem Reich mainly—although not entirely —during the 1930's. Orgone therapy, like Primal Therapy, is radical in nature, and the question naturally arises as to how they compare to each other. Since I have been a patient in both therapies—I saw an orgone therapist once a week for seven years and as of this writing have been in Primal Therapy several months—my experience in the two therapies may be useful as one basis for comparing them.

The similarities between the two therapies are easily stated. Both deal with the total psychobiological functioning of the individual. This sets both of them apart from most other therapies, since not only do they go beneath the intellectual and verbal level to the emotional, but they deal with feelings organismically, as they involve the entire functioning of the individual. The two therapies have a common aim: to remove as completely as possible the defense system, thus enabling the individual to function naturally. This aim requires the release of previously repressed feelings so that they can be freely expressed and the individual can experience them fully. The common aim also means fully trusting the self-regulatory capacity of the individual to run his own life. Primal Therapy and orgone therapy both set themselves to radically liberate the individual from his emotionally repressed condition.

To understand the differences between the two therapies it is first necessary to describe briefly orgone therapy (I assume the reader is already familiar with Primal Therapy), although it is impossible here to give more than a capsule sketch.[1] This can perhaps best be done by recounting the process by which Reich developed the therapy.

As a psychoanalyst in the 1920's Reich was impressed by the way attitudes characteristic of a given individual functioned as defenses against repressed feelings and sensations, and he worked out methods of analyzing these characterological defenses.[2] During the same period Reich was also convinced that the key to curing neurosis was the establishment by the patient of a satisfactory sexual relationship. He felt that the neurosis was energetically supported by the unreleased sexual emotions, and that if these were fully released the defense structure would collapse from lack of support.

During the 1930's Reich realized that the characterological defenses which defended the individual—and thus held back his sexual emotions from full release—involved chronic muscular tensions at various places in the organism which physically held back the awareness and expression of feelings. When parts of this muscular armor, as he came to call it, were released, the feelings whose denial had originally prompted the muscular constriction which had then become chronic expressed themselves spontan-

[1] A good introduction to Reich's work, both in psychiatry and in natural science, is his *Selected Writings* (New York: Farrar, Straus, and Giroux, 1960). A briefer introduction can be found in Ola Raknes' *Wilhelm Reich and Orgonomy* (New York: St. Martin's Press, 1970). His biophysical theory of neurosis is presented in *The Function of the Orgasm* (New York: Farrar, Straus, and Giroux, 1961), while a more recent presentation of the therapy is Elsworth F. Baker's *Man in the Trap* (New York: Macmillan, 1967).

[2] His book, *Character Analysis* (3d ed., New York: Farrar, Straus, and Giroux, 1970), the first edition of which was still in the analytic framework, has been widely used in psychoanalysis.

eously. Emotional disorder was rooted in the whole organism, and could be approached by biophysical work on the organism which resulted in simultaneous release of chronic muscular tensions and the associated dammed-up feelings. When through a systematic removal of the muscular armor feelings could move unimpeded through the organism the individual was also capable of full orgastic sexual release. At this point the energy supporting the neurosis was withdrawn, and this rechanneling of emotional energy made possible by the removal of muscular and emotional blocks enabled the individual to function in an "unarmored," natural manner. Those individuals who became capable of completely letting go of conscious control during intercourse and letting their feelings flow unimpeded throughout their bodies Reich called "orgastically potent." He took the achievement of this condition —rare in our sick, sexually repressive society—as the criterion of cure.

During the same years that Reich developed his biophysical therapy he also indentified the nature of the emotional energy whose liberation was the goal of his therapy. In the late 1930's he came to recognize this energy as distinct from any of the presently known forms of energy and as operative in all forms of life, and so gave it his own name: orgone energy. Reich developed an orgone box in which one sits in order to concentrate orgone energy— which he believed fills all space—so that it can heighten the energetic charge.

In the later years of Reich's life he made a number of discoveries concerning orgone energy, only one of which —in addition to the orgone accumulator—is relevant to his therapy. This discovery was that when orgone energy is immoblized, whether by confinement in a muscularly armored organism or by exposure in certain conditions to other energies such as radiation and electricity, it loses its life-enhancing quality and turns deadly. Reich called such immobilized orgone energy DOR—Deadly Orgone. To withdraw such energy from the organism, he developed a device which consists of a set of cables connected to an orgone accumulator, which in turn is connected by a cable to a water source. The DOR, attracted by water, is drawn off from the organism, thus allowing the immobilized orgone energy to flow more freely.

In my personal orgone therapy I worked with a very experienced therapist who has had the responsibility of training other orgone therapists for twenty years. In describing my therapy, it should be pointed out that it was not typical of most cases in that therapy. My therapist diagnosed me as a "neurotic with a schizophrenic core." This "schizophrenic core" made me a more difficult patient—indeed, it unltimately frustrated the whole therapy. Before entering orgone therapy I had had an extensive psychoanalysis which had removed some of my neurotic repressions without really affecting the deeper levels of my emotional disorder. My hope in entering orgone therapy was that its relatively nonverbal, biophysical approach could reach a level which psychoanalysis could not. I believe my therapy was also atypical in that there was relatively little release of feelings as contrasted with the dramatic case histories which can be found in the English-language orgonomic periodicals and books of the last thirty years.

A great deal of my time in orgone therapy was spent stretched out on a couch in my underpants breathing deeply. The scanty attire is to enable the therapist to see and work directly with the contracted muscles throughout the body. The deep breathing is to enable the organism to tolerate progressively higher charges of energy flowing throughout the body, thus lessening the need to hold this energy back by chronic muscular contractions. In understanding orgone therapy it is necessary to keep in mind that for Reich, emotion basically is life energy flowing through the organism, producing a variety of physiological effects. Since emotion and life energy are considered functionally identical, a release of either means the release of the other. The biophysical work, seeking to restore unimpeded energy flow, is thus at the same time seeking to restore full emotional awareness and expression. The breathing in itself often led in my therapy to some release of emotion.

In addition to the breathing, some time in each session was spent talking to the therapist. The purpose was not the therapist's making interpretations as in analysis—although I understand this is sometimes done—but rather clarification of the patient's situation, including dreams, the nature of neurosis and therapy, etc. Other techniques which were used included hitting the couch to release aggressive feelings, the manual pushing of the muscular armor by the therapist, and gagging every morning when one's stomach is empty to try to open the throat muscles. The accumulator was not prescribed.

Along with the breathing one was asked to roll one's eyes, and also to open and close them, as one breathed in and out. The purpose here was to increase the tolerance of the brain to energy flow, the brain and the optic nerve being essentially the same organ. Reich had become convinced that in schizophrenia one of the main ways of holding back the flow of emotional energy was through the contraction of the brain. Hence, my therapist spent much time attempting to mobilize my eyes as a way of mobilizing my brain as well.

Another method besides breathing of mobilizing one's eyes and brain, developed since Reich's death, was also used. This was the movement of the beam from a small pocket flashlight in my field of vision. I was to follow the light with my eyes. Sometimes, I understand, this method results in strong expressions of feeling. In my case this didn't occur. What did happen was that I had a slight retinal hemorrhage in my right eye, which was fortunately soon identified by my physician. While I can't be certain the photostimulation caused it, it seems probable. By this time in the therapy I had high blood pressure, which was probably due to the building up of emotional energy without adequate release. On learning of the retinal hemorrhage the photostimulation was stopped. The factor causing me to hold back emotionally was so tenacious that rather than yielding, the tissues began to break down.

Finally, after seven years of orgone therapy which were sustained by the belief that it was the deepest, most effective therapy I knew of, my patience ran out and I terminated the therapy. What were the results of these seven years? On the positive side, my vision had improved appreciably, as independently checked by an ophthalmologist before and after therapy. My lung capacity increased, as evidenced by my greater ease in breathing when hiking at high altitudes. My height increased one inch, presumably by the relaxation of certain muscles bending my back. I developed a greater acceptance of and identification with my body than previously. And more important than all of these, I began to have intercourse with girls for the first time in my life.

On the negative side, while my anxiety lessened in some situations, it didn't in others. I never came close to letting go completely biophysically or emotionally. At the end of my orgone therapy I still could not recall much of my childhood. Thus, important feelings from that time remained repressed. There was still a good deal of neurotic acting out. And my relationships with people remained difficult, with my spending too much time by myself and not regularly working. The problems which had prompted me to go into therapy—inability to feel, to relate to others satisfactorily, to really love, to work at something meaningful—all remained unsolved. The "schizophrenic core" had not been dissolved, and it was still wrecking my life.

What has happened to me thus far in the few months that I have been in Primal Therapy is that the nature of the underlying central block has been clarified, and a method of access which offers real hope of dissolving it has been provided.

In the first three weeks of intensive individual therapy, I believe it is accurate to state that I experienced more emotional release than during my entire orgone therapy. I cried in a deeper manner than ever before, both vocally and in organismic involvement. A film I saw during this period at the therapist's request was more emotionally meaningful than any film I have ever seen, because I was more emotionally open.

When Primal Therapy began to open me up more, whenever I began to feel intensely, the feelings would develop to a certain point at which I would begin to choke. The feelings were blocked by the constriction of my neck. My former therapist had recognized at the outset of my orgone therapy that my biophysical constriction was centered in my neck, and to a lesser extent my jaw and upper chest, as well as in my brain, but since these muscular contractions never really let go, the related emotion never came out, and what it was and why it was held back so tenaciously remained a puzzle.

Since it has emerged in Primal Therapy that birth experiences are often very influential in emotional disorder, I asked my mother what she remembered about my birth. Her reply was very enlightening. It seems that while a fetus in the uterus I had got the umbilical cord wrapped around my neck, and in my buttocks-down position this was preventing me from being born. The attending obstetrician had to turn me around in the uterus, using instruments for this purpose. A doctor assisting him stated later that it was only the obstetrician's skill which saved my life. As it was, it was a long and difficult delivery, and I came out with scars on my face and a bump on my head, both of which soon disappeared.

What did not disappear was the emotional consequences of this traumatic experience. Dr. Arthur Janov had seen that it was fear of strangulation which was blocking my intense feelings by constricting my throat, and when I told him about the strangulation trauma in the uterus he realized that it was there that the Primal split from my feelings had occurred. The terror of the experience had been too much for me as a still unborn infant to take, and I had shut off my feelings by constricting the neck muscles. The fear of reexperiencing this terror has kept them constricted ever since, thus effectively preventing normal emotional functioning. The essential nature of the central underlying block, which I have been trying to get at without success for many years, was thus rather rapidly experienced and identified in Primal Therapy.

The therapy also offers a way of dissolving the block, by going back to the feelings at that critical time and reexperiencing them bit by bit. This is very difficult to do, since the terror at that time was very great. As a not yet born infant I was, after all, exceptionally defenseless and vulnerable to so engulfing an experience. In therapy my body perspires all over when I begin to approach these feelings. However, it seems to me I allow strangulation feelings to develop more easily than early in therapy, and there is real hope of progressively overcoming the block.[3]

Since my own case is rather extreme and not typical, the case of another person might be briefly mentioned which illustrates another aspect of the differences between Primal and orgone therapy, that is, the question of how thorough orgone therapy is when the outcome is more favorable than mine. Dr. Theodore P. Wolfe, Reich's first American co-worker, was the man who facilitated Reich's move to this country in 1939. After therapy with Reich he worked as an orgone therapist, translated several of Reich's books from German to English, edited the first orgonomic periodical in English, and throughout the 1940's was one of the principal workers in orgonomy. As a biographical article by his wife, Gladys Meyer Wolfe, makes clear,[4] Wolfe was very considerably benefited by his orgone therapy, and Reich must have been relatively satisfied to give him the responsibilities that he did. Yet when Reich in the early 1950's rejected Wolfe, an old predisposition to tuberculosis became activated, and four years later, while still in his early fifties, Wolfe was dead. From a Primal point of view the inference is inevitable that Reich was Wolfe's surrogate father, and when this surrogate father rejected him it reactivated the unresolved pain concerning Wolfe's actual father (who was Germanic, cold, and distant), and the resultant pain was so great it killed him. Orgone therapy had biophysically

[3] It does not appear that obstetricians are aware of the emotional consequences of umbilical cord strangulation. M. F. Ashley Montague in his *Prenatal Influences* (Springfield, Ill.: Charles C Thomas, 1962), a comprehensive survey of the effects of prenatal development on later life, does not mention umbilical cord strangulation, although he does mention the evidence pointing toward anoxia in some cases of schizophrenia, mental retardation, epilepsy, and cerebral palsy. If doctors were fully aware of the consequences of umbilical cord strangulation, one wonders whether they couldn't routinely check on whether the cord was wrapped around the infant's neck, whether by palpation or some other method, and perform a caesarean in such cases, and if this were accompanied by a breech-birth position, which seems to make such placement of the cord particularly hazardous, perform a caesarean.

[4] *The Journal of Orgonomy*, Vol. 4 (1970).

opened Wolfe up considerably, but it had never enabled him adequately to resolve his Primal Pains. While a reading of orgonomic case histories makes clear that Primal Pains are often reexperienced in orgone therapy when muscular blocks dissolve, including birth experiences at times, one wonders whether all the individual's Primal Pains are ever thoroughly connected, since the focus of the therapy lies elsewhere. The substantial changes which many individuals do undergo in orgone therapy probably result from the considerable reexperiencing of Primal Pain which often occurs with the dissolution of biophysical armor. But since orgone therapy regards this reexperiencing of past events as only a concomitant of the process of biophysical opening and release which is the central stress of the therapy, there is no attempt to have the individual go thoroughly and deeply into all significant Primal Pains. In Wolfe's case it seems probable that some very significant pains weren't gone into enough to fully connect with and thus deactivate them.

The basic difference between orgone and Primal therapies would seem to be this: orgone therapy is primarily a biophysical therapy which seeks to release muscular contractions and thereby enable emotional energy to flow freely, whereas Primal Therapy is primarily an experiential therapy which seeks to enable the individual to connect with his repressed feelings and thereby to release chronic muscular contractions. The two therapies are working at the same psychobiological problem with similar objectives but from opposite sides. Thus there is much congruence, but also important differences. The experiential focus of Primal Therapy deals more directly with the causes of emotional disorder, which are themselves emotional experiences which cannot be accepted and so must be repressed, than does the biophysical focus of orgone therapy, which centers on the physiological mechanisms of that repression. Orgone therapy seeks the release of emotional energy per se, believing that a biophysically open organism is necessarily an emotionally healthy one. Primal Therapy seeks to connect the individual with all significant repressed feelings, believing that only when all the principal Primal Pains are experienced can defenses be fully discarded and natural functioning attained. Orgone therapy stresses full sexual release as the crux of biophysical openness and natural functioning, while Primal Therapy concerns itself equally with all repressed feelings.

The experiential focus of Primal Therapy enables deeply-lying trauma to be identified in cases in which orgone therapy cannot budge the biophysical defense—as my own case illustrates. It also enables a far more thorough resolution of Primal Pains—as can be seen negatively in the case of Dr. Wolfe. The experiential focus of Primal Therapy, lying closer to basic causes, enables most patients to be cured more rapidly and more thoroughly. Further, medical training isn't necessary in order to practice the therapy, as is the case with orgone therapy. In summary, of the two radical therapies, Primal Therapy offers the more effective means of liberating people to live.

3. MY EXPERIENCE WITH ORGONE THERAPY

Sally

I first entered orgone therapy in a state of total confusion, hysteria, and near-panic. My thoughts and feelings were very conflicting, and this was tortuous. The doctor suggested that it would be more profitable if both my husband and I came for treatment. My first treatments were an effort to get me out of the panic I was in; therefore, my memory is rather vague in regard to the first few weeks or months. The usual routine, however, was to enter a room and disrobe; everything came off except for my underpants. I would lie on a couch, and the therapist would sit in a chair at the side of the bed. My knees would be raised with my feet together while lying down, as this enabled the therapist to be aware of any tension or changes in the legs. If any clothing was tight enough to leave a mark on the body, it was *too* tight, and I was not to wear tight clothing. I was told to gag every day by sticking my finger down my throat; also I was to have one ounce of liquor each day.

The procedure was pretty nearly the same each session, and it was one that was used to help break down muscular armor or defenses. The doctor stimulated my eyes by moving his finger back and forth and in a circular motion above them. Certain muscle groups were overstimulated by punching. At times he would overstimulate the duodenum by punching me with his thumb or finger. I was not told why all this was being done until much later when changes began to take place. All of this helped to relieve anxiety. At first I went twice a week, and later cut it to once a week. I was asked to talk about my past and present life, and how I felt about it. We talked about mother, father, child rearing, everyday living, and God.

If there were incidents in my past or present that were disturbing, I was helped to relieve my anxiety about them. For instance, there was a particular incident in my life that took place when I was six or seven years old. My uncle was janitor of the grade school I attended. He would lure me into his storage room by offering me chewing gum or candy. At the time he would grab me and proceed to kiss me and fondle me sexually. My therapist felt this incident was responsible for my frigidity, so that particular scene was reenacted by his pretending to be my uncle. This was repeated many times throughout the five years I went to him. This treatment must have been helpful to me because I *did* lose some of my fear concerning sex. I did not, however, at any time lose all my fear. I was still afraid to reach out or express desire for affection. My feeling since entering Primal Therapy is that my frigidity started long before the incident with my uncle.

If the therapist sensed fear or anger from me over something I was discussing he would attempt to get my feelings out by reenacting the scene. If it was anger over a situation he would have me hit the bed to express that anger. If it was fear or frustration, it was discussed and usually ended in a crying scene. Everything that I experienced or discussed while in therapy was brought out by my therapist. Often these experiences would seem silly, puzzling, and even embarrassing.

Even though I felt helped by this therapy, I also felt that I was becoming dependent on it, and that in order to stay reasonably well I would have to go continuously. This feeling was disturbing to me, but it proved to be a valid one, for within a period of less than five years I was pretty much back into my old feelings and problems.

The main difference to me between Primal Therapy and orgone therapy was the total destruction of my defenses by seeing my Primal Therapist daily for the first three weeks. Perhaps the most important thing is that I feel my own pain when and if I am ready for it. I now believe there is no significance in reenacting an incident if I am not really into the feeling of it. It only becomes playacting, and in this way any patient can avoid really feeling his pain forever. When I saw the orgone therapist only once a week I soon learned how to fool him, and myself. In Primal Therapy I am more on my own, feeling my own pain when and if I am ready. My contact with a therapist is close, so there is less opportunity for games. I want to progress for my own welfare, not because it pleases a therapist.

The group sessions are extremely valuable because I learn to relate to other people. It helps give me insight into my own problems as well as those of others. I realize I am not alone in my struggle, though in one sense I will always be alone. My struggle is hard to give up as I often feel comfortable in it; it has been the only way I've known. Hearing and seeing other people progress gives me courage.

After only a few weeks of Primal Therapy I have much more self-awareness; I feel secure with my feelings, that they are real. For the first time I know what is really happening to me and why. The changes I feel don't seem puzzling and mysterious, as they did with orgone therapy. I have much more understanding about what I feel happening to me.

The constant outside stimulation of the muscle groups in orgone therapy helped tear down my physical armor or tension, but did nothing to help me connect my need for defense or bodily armor, and the tension returned because no real connection was made. The result was that no basic changes in behavior occurred. In other words, the old fears and hurts were still there.

In orgone therapy the physical changes that took place were frightening because they did not accompany any real understanding. It seems to me the therapy would have to fail in the long run and result in total dependency on the therapist.

V. Research

1. INTRODUCTION

There are essentially two ways to validate progress in psychotherapy: to test what the mind says and to test what the body says. Mind tests are called psychological tests—such as the Rorschach, sentence completion, and Thematic Apperception Tests. Body tests are called physiological measurements—such as heart rate, pulse and body temperature. I believe that there can be no psychological validity without an accompanying physiological one. No matter what the mind says, if the body is still registering tension, the person is not well. Conversely, if the body has a low tension level but the person feels bad, he is still not well. To repeat an old theme, we are a unit, and though we may separate that unit for purposes of study (psychological-physiological), we must be careful not to reify our abstractions.

In the quasi-religious "Science of Mind" movement, there are thousands of people who have convinced themselves that they never felt better. If they were measured with sophisticated electronic measurements to determine tension levels, we might find that their minds were quite at odds with their bodily states. Are they well? Is one well if he thinks he is? No. You are well if your entire organism says so, and only then.

To that end, the Primal Institute has recently established a research laboratory with electronic instruments to measure many aspects of physiological functioning. In addition, we are computerizing brain-wave tests so that fine measurements can be made of changes in brain-wave functioning. We are conducting interviews on a random sample basis with patients who have had five or more months of Primal Therapy. These are in-depth interviews running an hour or more which aim at eliciting the subjective feelings of patients. Here we are interested in changes in symptoms as observed by the patient himself. The fact that symptoms disappear is highly significant, yet it is only part of the story, for often it is possible for the therapy to drain off enough tension to make symptoms go away. What we are interested in knowing, then, is whether a high level of residual tension remains after the disappearance of the symptom. If this is so, then the symptom may well return under stress. If the tension level is continuously low, we can feel safer in saying that the symptom seems to be gone for good—is cured.

Subjective reports are crucial and should not be dismissed as "unobjective evidence." The fact that an epileptic has no more seizures is an important statistic—an objective fact, as it were. But when he also says, "I know now what my epilepsy is all about and I know exactly how to prevent seizures," that, too, is significant evidence; particularly when he can, indeed, control and prevent seizures. Just because an outsider is making judgments and writing numbers about another person does not make the evidence objective. A psychoanalyst judging a book on Primal Therapy is not necessarily objective because he is subjectively uninvolved in Primal Therapy. His viewpoint is colored by his subjective state, his adherence to a school of therapy, and other factors. Detachment does not equal objectivity. Objectivity is the ability to be clear to see and judge reality. I submit that a truly objective person is one whose subjective Pains are resolved so that he can see reality for what it is. Such a person will be objective. A post-Primal patient is probably the most objective viewer of his progress. How can an outsider measure the depths of his pre-Primal depressions, the ferocity of his previous headaches, and the heartache of losing his wife and children?

In dialectic fashion, the most subjective person, the one who has experienced most of himself, becomes objective; while the detached (from himself) individual becomes subject to that hidden self, "subjective." That subjective force colors his choice of research area, the data he considers relevant, and the interpretations he makes of the information. It may also cause him to make no interpretation (out of unconscious fear) because that would bring him into the area of ideas and opinions. Thus, as often happens, each research finding is left to flounder on its own. The result is thousands of research projects each year unconnected to one another, unattached to any cohesive theory which could integrate and make sense out of them. The Primal definition of objectivity is the confluence of conscious and unconscious. So long as significant unconscious forces are shielded from consciousness, there can be no objectivity. When the self is at once both subject and object—when no part of oneself is an object detached from subjective experience—then we are objective and the experience reported by an objective self is valid and objective.

We see this change from subjectivity to objectivity in our Primal parents who, before therapy, were so involved with themselves, so detached from their children, that they could not be objective about their children's suffering. After therapy, they see those children clearly and objectively. Sometimes social scientists forget that they themselves are part of the data in their research. They select and influence results, particularly in the realm of psychotherapy. They become a variable to be accounted for. I want to stress that unemotionality does not make objectivity; quite the opposite, it makes for neurosis. As our research progresses we may be able to quantify objectivity. We are finding that brain waves are part of the defense structure. In neurotics, when the wave frequency is diminished by artificial means such as meditation, there is a counterbalancing increase in the amplitude of the wave. That is, the less controlled the brain, the more open it is to Primal memory circuits and the greater the Primal input—pulsing the brain toward higher amplitude. In our framework, it means a more repressed system and defended brain. Amplitude is a literal function of the amount of neurons firing. The more Pain being repressed, the greater the number of activated neurons required. Neurotics have a much busier brain. It is therefore a brain that is more distractable, less able to concentrate, and more difficult to put to sleep. We are finding in our initial samplings that amplitude is a key indicator of repression—and neurosis.

A defended brain is an unobjective one. We would expect, therefore, that as both the frequency and the amplitude decrease, as it does in Primal patients, the person would become more objective; this is what patients report. They know what is "their" thing from that of others. They know when someone is projecting his neurosis onto them and no longer become enmeshed in it. As they become one, they can separate the outside world from the inside one. No matter what a person says about how feeling he is, the EEG pattern may provide more accurate information in this regard. Our hypothesis is that a feeling person is "low and slow" in brain-wave profiles.

What is the importance of research in our therapy? We need to know that this is all not self-delusion; that when people feel better and lose their symptoms the changes are truly reflected in their bodily states. We watch the progress of an epileptic (and nonepileptics) and see that brain waves do change in predictable directions along with lower blood pressure, heart rate, and so on.

It is rather amazing to me that everywhere in the world there are therapists treating patients every day with no idea at all of how these patients are doing physiologically. Therapists may be in practice for decades and not once know for sure if they are doing patients any good.

The same problem obtains in the matter of psychiatric evaluation. When a person goes to a psychiatrist for an evaluation what gets evaluated? The defense, not the bodily state. A person with a good, socially approved, intellectual defense may come out with a good evaluation, while a person whose defenses are not working does not fare so well on the psychiatric report. Who is sicker?

We have placed our faith in experts rather than ourselves; and the experts have placed their faith in numbers and categories. How much expertise does it take to know that crying babies must be picked up? About the same amount as it does to know that war is bad. What statistics prove that we need to pick up crying babies or that war is bad? Feeling people know the answer because they can feel their experience and learn from it. Neurotics cannot learn from experience because they don't experience; they assemble data—to prove what can't be felt.

Why haven't hundreds of thousands of statistical studies in the social sciences over the past half century produced a cure for neurosis or even brought us close? The flaw, I believe, is in the mistaken notion that truth is statistical instead of biological. We have relied on abstractions. Meanwhile, the major leaps that have taken place in the field have been made by the speculators and theoreticians, those not satisfied with quantification. It is almost impossible to place a speculative article (as opposed to statistical) in a professional journal today. There is little room for ideas in a field crowded with statistics.

Scientists want more evidence as to the efficacy of Primal Therapy, and rightly so. But what constitutes evidence is the question.

Is evidence only objective numbers on a graph, or can feelings be evidence? Certainly, feelings to the person experiencing them are facts enough. Those felings form part of the validation. Several scientists about to enter Primal Therapy have asked for more research data before entering. After one Primal, they are no longer interested in "objective" data because the intense internal experience provided them with the only significant data they needed.

Why has the field been so loath to consider feelings as proper evidence? From a psychological point of view, one reason is that we have been brought up to believe that (our) feelings don't count. It isn't enough to say to our parents, "I am going to do such and such just because I *feel* like it." Usually, we have to justify it, offer reasons and evidence for wanting to do something. So we get stuck on the need for evidence.

Is evidence what a group of "experts" agree on? Does consensus among neurotic social scientists validate? Psychoanalysis is a case in point. Thousands of analysts agree on the validity of psychoanalytic therapy; otherwise, I assume, they would not be doing it. Decades of "objective" analytic research has changed the theory and the therapy little. Why? Because the data is interpreted psychoanalytically—a circular affair. For example, one index of maturity in analytic theory is the ability to postpone gratification. So when a person reports that he can do that, the analytic researcher would score a point on the maturity scale. I don't happen to think that delaying enjoyment is maturity; I think it is neurosis. But in analytic research the postponement of gratification would, in circular fashion, constitute objective data and help validate the theory.

Research in conditioning therapy often results in sophisticated statistics. But to what data are the statistics applied? Behavior. Not data dealing with feelings and internal states. Thus behavioral data reify and validate behavioral theory. These scientists are called "behavioral scientists," which already indicates which pieces of data will be investigated as important and relevant.

How does one indicate to these two disparate theoretical research groups that the data they are seeking is wrong? If behavior alone is the sine qua non, little can be done, because nonbehavioral data is considered irrelevant. Thus in conditioning (behavioral) research, how one *behaves* after therapy would be the thing to be measured, and the statistics on behavior would help validate the theory again. Behavior therapists look at behavior, and the best their patients can do is "behave." Analysts attend predominantly to what their patients say, and these patients say, eventually, what the analyst (and the patient) needs to hear. Both are obsolete because they fragment human beings in order to achieve self-fulfilling predictions.

Scientific evidence is that which can be replicated—duplicated exactly. Thus, if a therapy is scientific, the results should obtain time and time again. Unfortunately, most of the therapy done today depends very much on the personality of the therapist. It has become an art *because it has not been a science.* Primal Therapy is replicated daily. We achieve the same results irrespective of which therapist is involved, so long as he is trained and competent, and these results are measured with each patient.

We have previously relied heavily on "control groups" for our data—matching one group (say, with therapy) against a similar group (without therapy)—to make our findings. The problem with control groups is that human beings are not duplicable. Nor is their history duplicable. The only real control that can be used in obtaining psychological data is the patient himself, before and after therapy. The control is individual and specific.

One wonders if we have not raised the neurotic virtues of skepticism, caution, and objectivity to the level of a scientific principle, so that social science in some ways mirrors our neuroses. We have so left our bodies behind in the search for objective truth that we forget that if something feels true it is likely to *be* true. We have relied on numbers and statistics because we don't feel—because we cannot be properly subjective—and there will never be enough statistics to prove to an unfeeling person what feelings are about.

Scientific skepticism is often a worthwhile virtue; it prevents jumping to unwarranted conclusions. Unfortunately, that skepticism which takes the form of "We can't really be sure" (about anything) is often a cover for the inability to be sure of oneself, about anything. Thus the insecure person becomes content to gather information and more information as ends in themselves, thereby forestalling any need to come to a conclusion.

This same skepticism leads the supercautious scientist to ask for more time, and more time. He wants to see how something does over the long haul before making a final judgment; an admirable quality. But too often "time" becomes apotheosized as though there were some magic about it. Long-range studies need not prove anything if the basis for the research is wrong. For example, a Behavior therapist may shock an overeater over a period of months while setting tasty morsels in front of him. This conditioning process continues until the person no longer "wants" to eat. He may lose weight and stay thin for two years. A long-range study of the efficacy of Conditioning therapy for overeating may provide validation for the method. But what does that number "two" (years) mean? Very little if not tied to biologic data. He may be thinner but in the long run much more susceptible to coronary attack owing to increased tension.

Research findings become the *summum bonum* in an authoritarian society because neurosis means to trust mental abstractions instead of one's body and its feelings. In authoritarian society, we learn to trust experts—the elite, both politically and psychologically. Only "qualified" people may make judgments about your state of mental health. And what qualifies these experts? Too often, the study of philosophy, theory, and statistics. Having spent years studying outmoded theories, the graduate therapist may now make pronouncements about who is well and who is sick.

The research studies which follow are neither more important nor more objective than the case reports cited elsewhere in this book. They simply provide different kinds of evidence for the effectiveness of Primal Therapy.

The subsequent two sections, in turn, study the post-Primal patient psychologically and physiologically. The results should converge and be in accord with one another. We cannot have so-called valid psychological findings when the physiological correlates diverge. Though we split up the patient for purposes of study into the psychological and physiological, we must keep in mind data can be truly valid. In reality, there is no *psychologic* behavior; there can only be *psychobiologic* behavior.

2. FOLLOW-UP STUDIES OF PRIMAL PATIENTS

A systematic follow-up program of investigation of Primal patients was recently begun. The following are the preliminary results from a sample study of twenty-five Primal patients who have had five or more months of Primal Therapy. We studied patients who are still in therapy and those who have been out for as long as three years. These patients were given questionnaires to fill out and had one-hour taped interviews with the investigator. Sample transcripts of these interviews are found in the Appendix. Questions on the questionnaire were as follows:

1. How long in therapy? How often did you come to group after three weeks?

2. Have you been cured, partially cured, helped, the same, or worse? Explain.
3. Any specific ailments relieved or cured?
4. What previous therapy have you had?
5. Would you ever enter another kind of therapy?
6. What specifically about Primal Therapy helped you?
7. What criticisms do you have of Primal Therapy? How would you improve it?
8. Would you recommend it to others?
9. How has your behavior and life style changed?
10. Do you still Primal? How often?
11. Do you now smoke, drink, take drugs, or overeat? Explain.
12. Do you feel the need for the above?
13. Describe your sex life.
14. Describe your everyday life (job, family, kids, etc.).

Because "cure" is always an individual matter, it was difficult to make a simple tabulation of answers to some of the questions. In those cases I will provide a sample of the kinds of answers received. On two questions there was 100 percent agreement: question number five, "Would you ever enter another kind of therapy?" The answer was "no." On question number eight, "Would you recommend it to others?" the answer was again a unanimous "yes." However, there was a qualification. Nearly all respondents said that they would never struggle to convince anyone about the therapy. They would simply recommend it and let it go at that.

The age range of these patients is twenty-four to fifty-four. Seven were in their twenties, twelve were in their thirties, the remainder were in their forties except one in his fifties. Six were previously divorced, thirteen were married, and six were single. There were thirteen females and twelve males.

How long in therapy? How often did you come to group after three weeks?

Fifty percent of the respondents had between five and eight months of treatment. Fifteen percent had eight months to one year, 30 percent had one year to one and one-half years, and 5 percent had two years or more. Many of the respondents still believed they were in therapy even though they came only occasionally when they needed to Primal. One of the benefits, they say, of Primal Therapy is that you can come almost any time and Primal in a group. Thus it is most difficult to say who is a patient and who is not. Beginning patients usually come to group three times a week for the first four or five months. Later on, they may come once every three months. My observation is that the general turning point in therapy occurs between six and eight months. This is the point of "no return," when the patient is wide open and unable to go back and be neurotic even if he wanted to. From then on, it is only a matter of continuing to Primal either at home or occasionally in group, or both. I would say that the major work in breaking down defenses takes place in the first six months. There are cases, however, in which eighteen months may be consumed in this process.

Thus in question ten, "Do you still Primal?" nearly all patients, in or out of therapy, said yes. The frequency is several times a week for beginning patients, weekly for patients after the eighth month, and once every month or two for the rest. By the eighth month, patients most often will say, "I know when I'm feeling, when I'm blocking, and how to get to these feelings immediately. I don't put off my Pain."

Have you been cured, partially cured, helped, the same, or worse? Explain.

"Cured" is defined as having either no more Primals or Primaling rarely. This means little or no residual pain. Three felt cured. They were also the ones who were out of treatment the longest—two and three years.

"Partially cured" is defined as mostly tension-free, Primaling periodically whenever tension arises. "Helped" was defined as still acting out on occasion instead of feeling. All subjects except one believed that they were partially cured. The one who felt helped was in her fifth month of therapy. No one reported being the same or worse.

The statement many made was that they see an end to therapy but not to the Pain. They believe the Primals are a style of life, and that chances are they will continue to Primal for many years to come. Our future follow-up studies will investigate that. No one doubts that this is the cure, the only kind of therapy for the treatment of mental illness, but they question when, if ever, a full cure takes place.

Any specific ailments relieved or cured?

I am going to list exactly the ailments which have been eliminated, according to the statements of twenty-five patients: high blood pressure, high pulse rate, arthritis, hypothyroidism, constipation, headaches, allergies, backaches, colitis, peptic ulcers, dizziness, alcoholism, menstrual cramps, skin disorders, hemorrhoids, stomach pains, nausea, and teeth grinding. The highest concentration of complaints eliminated comprised stomach disorders and headaches. I hesitate to write a list like the above because it makes Primal Therapy sound like a panacea. What we need to understand is that as tension builds over our early development, it puts increased pressure on our biological systems so that the weakest point will be affected. When tension lifts, it would be expected that whatever symptoms occurred because of the previous internal pressure would vanish—unless, of course, there has been endorgan damage. We cannot rebuild damaged tissue. Blood pressure is not immediately reduced except in occasional situations; it is a more long-range process in which the reduction comes after several months of treatment. The same is true of hypothyroidism. Cure here is not only a subjective feeling, in terms of the patient's having none of the usual symptoms when off medication, but also of medical laboratory studies which indicate changes in thyroid output.

Menstrual cramps are a frequent beginning complaint in women, and within the first months of therapy they usually report none of the previous need for medication to ease menstrual problems. Arthritis is the most interesting change. The woman who had it said that she had been stiffened against the Pain so long she wasn't aware of what she was doing until in a Primal she felt herself stiffen against the onrushing Pain and develop arthritic symptoms. She later said that her joints feel "lubricated" for the first time in years.

Generally, my clinical observation is that the more repressed the individual, the deeper in his body lie the symptoms. I have found that people who came in with the initial complaint of a stomach disorder would develop a skin rash as the Pain was "coming to the surface." Those with colitis are usually the most repressed of my patients.

What previous therapy have you had?

Again, I am quoting only the kinds of therapy these twenty-five patients had previously undergone: transactional analysis, psychoanalysis, group encounter, bioenergetics, Reichian therapy, Rogerian, Gestalt, Rolfing, marriage counseling, Synanon, and eclectic, insight therapy. Many had been psychoanalyzed. Second came group encounter therapy (as in the various Growth Centers), and third was eclectic, insight therapy.

The length of time these patients had been in treatment ranged from three months to thirteen years. The longest period of time spent was in psychoanalysis and bioenergetics. The average length of time spent was three and a half years. The total amount of previous therapy for these twenty-five patients was seventy-six years. Three had had no previous therapy.

Many patients who had been psychoanalyzed did honestly believe they were helped. The same is true with many of the other therapies. It was only after the return of a symptom or a specific crisis in their lives that they decided to enter Primal Therapy, and it was only after several Primals that they understood the profound differences between this and other forms of treatment. That is why they all say, emphatically, that they would never consider another form of therapy.

What specifically about Primal Therapy helped you?

The answers here fell into three groups: 1. Getting in touch with my feelings. 2. Feeling the past so it won't hinder the present. 3. Having everything I do accepted in the therapy. This was an important factor. Wailing, letting out one's rage, being infantile, all were accepted and understood. Each respondent said in one way or another that he was finally getting to the "walled-off" self. They respected the fact that there was someone around who could make them feel safe to feel.

What criticisms do you have of Primal Therapy? How would you improve it?

We were gratified to find that most criticisms of the therapy were minor. Of course, we did not poll those who had been removed from Primal Therapy (about 2 percent) who might have different ideas. Causes for removal, incidentally, usually involve violation of the rules, such as taking drugs, smoking, betraying group confidences, and so on. This group would make a good study sample later on.

Most of the criticisms centered on the lack of room in group and the noise there. Several felt we should take younger people. Other complaints in order of importance were: 1. Need more facilities and more therapists. 2. Keep closer tabs on patients later on. 3. Be more selective in choosing patients. 4. Too expensive. 5. Need a Primal house and a Primal community so that therapy can be done on an impatient basis, and so that post-Primal patients won't have to live isolated in the unreal world.

We try very hard to correct the criticisms. For example, once every six months we stop taking new patients and give old patients an extra week of individual therapy when requested. It has been most helpful. We continually add extra groups and train new therapists, but that training takes a long time, no matter how experienced the therapist had been, so we do lag behind. Criticisms about soundproofing nudged us to hire specialists who have done everything modern science can think of to soundproof our therapy rooms. Complaints are also made about the scarcity of female therapists. This is something we are trying to correct. But there are far fewer female psychologists and psychiatrists in practice. I think that we should try to form a Primal community, but we can't do it all. Patients will have to make their way in a world I didn't create and which I cannot control. We must all live under the system as best we can until there are enough well people to change it.

How has your behavior and life style changed?

This was the kind of question whose answers could not be easily tabulated. Changes depended on pre-Primal behavior. There are clusters of answers, however. The most significant change, all agreed, was the lack of tension and how this had changed their lives. With no tension, there was no need to act out relief habits such as smoking, drinking, masturbation, etc. With no tension, there were scarcely any psychosomatic symptoms.

Almost all respondents indicated that they no longer engaged in struggles anywhere. The implications of this vary. For example, those who were politically active are far less so now. They state that they are no longer "burning to save the world." Those who used to struggle with traffic to go to football games will no longer do so. There is no longer the struggle with one's parents, with far less parental contact. In some cases, however, patients report that they are closer to their parents because they are no longer trying to convert them into someone they need. They can relax and be less demanding with them.

The third cluster concerned pills. It seems that nearly all of the patients were on heavy medication before therapy. Some took as many as eight Seconals a day (which, I'm sure, would be a near-fatal dose for them now). Others were on six to ten aspirins a day or tranquilizers, sleeping pills, muscle relaxants, anti-depressants. All are completely off pills and feel no need for them at all.

The fourth cluster came with marriage and children. All claim excellent marital adjustment and being good relaxed parents.

Marital adjustment means rare arguments, few demands on one another, and better cooperation about all aspects of house and child care, because neither is a parent to the other but an equal partner. Women find a new interest in the simplest pleasures. Cooking takes on a feeling of art for some; others no longer want to cook at all. If a person was a compulsive "mother," cooking and cleaning compulsively before, this person is likely to give it up after therapy. "Cured" means being neither an efficient housekeeper nor a rotten one; it only means something in terms of the person's previous life style. Thus, no generalizations can be made about the meaning of cure other than the elimination of tension.

Women no longer feel they are "mothers." They are just people helping other people such as their children. There is no role for them in life other than just living. It seems to be relaxing to be just a person instead of an abstraction such as "mother." This new orientation enables them to make far fewer demands on their children such as keeping their rooms neat and orderly. Because of this lack of role playing, either husband or wife can work and earn a living. There is no "breadwinner." There is no "big daddy" earning and parceling out money to the infantilized wife.

I will list the rest of the statements in terms of frequency of response (called "Q-sort," in psychology):

1. I feel alive, yet calm and content.
2. My life is simpler. I do less, go less, want less, talk less; everything is less.
3. I trust my feelings now rather than others' opinions.
4. No one can push me around.
5. I am more patient and tolerant and don't blow up with sick people because I know they are only victims.
6. I am never depressed or moody.
7. I am no longer compulsive about anything.
8. I can finally sustain a relationship. Anxiety no longer drives me from one person to another.
9. I can see into people, their needs and their Pain.
10. I am less rigid.
11. I am alone a lot more.

12. I don't get sucked into other people's struggles.
13. My face has changed. I stand and walk differently.
14. I am no longer violent.
15. I can differentiate real from petty problems, and I don't take on impossible projects; I finish what I start.
16. I can concentrate now.
17. I can accept but don't need compliments.
18. I sing better, play chess better.
19. I have no more hallucinations.
20. I don't pick up stray animals.
21. I eat only natural foods.

One can see the great range of responses. To one person, "less rigid" means that his handwriting is freer. To another it means that he doesn't have to eat on the exact minute any more. Still another means that he can change his mind easily when the occasion demands. Here we note that even when we get the same response, "less rigid," it can mean something entirely different to each person. Thus, standard research, in which scales are drawn up in terms of flexibility, rigidity, etc., have little meaning unless they are individualized. When they are individualized, we see immediately that "rigid" has no universal meaning and that, in fact, each "rigid" response is different from any other "rigid" response. Thus there is no way to have a meaningful category of "rigid."

The response "I can concentrate" has a myriad of meanings (and, again, it is the *meaning* which is the real response). One person said that he could play better chess because he concentrated on the game instead of on "winning." Another said that she was no longer flighty and distractable because tension wasn't driving her mind in several different directions.

One of the changes which occurs with regularity is the move to natural foods. Many Post-Primal patients cannot eat unreal, processed foods. Their bodies won't accept it. It seems that a real bodily system rejects what is unreal in a literal way. The patients are not messianic about their dietary habits; they just select what they eat carefully.

Overall, one gets a feeling from these people that they do what they want, whenever possible. They are quite healthy and lead much simpler lives. The result is the virtual elimination of the demands on their children to perform and achieve.

Do you now smoke, drink, take drugs, or overeat? Explain.

Three still smoke occasionally. They cite as the reason having to work at unreal jobs which makes life unbearable and tension rise. Or they have been given permission to smoke while in therapy owing to the extrordinary Pain they suffer; this is especially true of those brought up in institutions. Of the rest of the sample, none smokes or drinks, yet some 90 percent reported smoking between one and a half to three packs per day before therapy (and after their previous therapy). These respondents indicated no desire to smoke. Those who drank once consumed up to one quart a day. About 20 percent were drinkers. None of them drinks now or indicates a desire for alcohol.

Overeating is another matter. Four respondents still said they eat too much. They explain that it is the last thing they are going to give up. One rationalized that he he didn't eat too much; it is simply that modern man cannot get the kind of exercise he needs to burn up what he eats. Whatever the explanation, some patients still do eat a great deal. None is terribly overweight or obese, but they do like to eat. One explanation is the almost unanimous fact that all were schedule-fed and "starved" as infants. It is also possible that because patients are wide open, feelings ascend "out of control." When patients attempt to inhibit these feelings with food, then eating becomes, in an almost literal way, "eating their feelings."

In regard to drugs, none of the patients reports the need for any drugs, including aspirins. However, four use marihuana occasionally; most of these say that they take it when they need to get to a feeling they are having trouble with. Others say they take it after a week of steady Primasl, when they want escape from the Pain for a time. Evidently, these patients can direct their trips very well; they can use pot to make themselves feel better or worse.

Describe your sex life.

Nearly all respondents said that they had much less sex than before. They added that the sex they do have is much deeper and more satisfying. Women report deeper and longer-lasting orgasms, while men report the elimination of premature ejaculation. Those still in therapy have much less sex than those out. This seems to be because these patients are still into their early presexual childhood. Later on, the frequency of sex picks up, but not much. Average frequency is once a week for those out of therapy; every other week for those still in. Nobody said he missed sex. Women seemed to feel that real sex interest occurs no more frequently than twice a month; that is, the sex interest follows the hormone cycle in relation to the menstrual period. Greatest interest shown was just before the onset of the period. When tension is cleared out of the system and no longer contaminates sex need, there is little doubt that there is a drop in sexual interest.

We are finding that frigidity is one of the most difficult problems to treat. It is usually the last symptom to go in Primal Therapy. The reason seems to be that *any* residual shutdown of the body owing to any kind of pain is reflected vaginally, producing frigidity. Once freed of that, patients report orgasms with their "whole body." When there is residual Pain, a number of patients report going straight into a Primal immediately after orgasm. The explanation seems to be that feeling anything deeply brings up the Pain. The usual answer to the question about sex life is that patients never knew what sex really was before because it was nearly all tension relief. One significant change noted is that after orgasm there is no longer that letdown feeling they used to have. Explanations of this seem to be that no longer do they have false expectations of sex.

Two homosexuals in the subject group said they were no longer homosexual.

Describe your everyday life (job, family, kids, etc.).

This is related to the question about how one's life style has changed. By and large, post-Primal patients see a lot of movies, listen to music, and take walks.

One Ph.D. candidate in English literature now reads only fairy tales and enjoys them. She no longer is interested in struggling with "profound" works of literature.

Social life is at a minimum—there are few if any dinner parties, nightclubs, etc. Younger people attend many rock concerts. They refuse to do what is painful, so they have given up all unreal relationships. They give up church, as well. All but one, who is still in therapy, report no need for religion. The general life style is living "out of the feelings" instead of cultural expectations. In terms of jobs, they usually decide that it doesn't matter what one does as long as one has oneself, so they don't feel committed on a lifelong basis to any job. In any other therapy, this would scarcely be considered normalcy or adjustment. Length of stay on the job is usually labeled "stability" and is a plus factor. In Primal Therapy it is neither plus nor minus. Jobs for most of the respondents, unless they are doing something real, is just a way to make money to enable them to do what they really want.

Most respondents claimed that the changes they made were mostly "inside" and could not be "viewed" or measured by anyone else. Indeed, the fact that they "lie around a lot" might well be viewed as pathologic by other research investigators. Natural man, it seems, is nonindustrial, noncompulsive and nondriving, "unambitious" in the neurotic sense, and simple. That inner state that cannot be "objectively" viewed is called "content." Being "calm" is a deceptive state, however, since many of these individuals appeared calm before therapy; only there was a raging tornado inside.

The tension these people report comes from their work situations, by and large. Many of them have no recourse but to work in unreal jobs in order to support their families, and that produces *current* tension. However, feeling apart from others' neuroses enables them not to be undone by the boss's sickness and his tirades. Teachers are no longer cowed by the school administrators, and parents no longer live through their children. There is no false hope in a job, in children, or in school and its higher degrees.

Most married couples do not want children. Having never lived for themselves, they are anxious to do so now. There are exceptions, however. The general tone is: "I am happy being who I am and what I am, and that's all that counts."

So the composite Primal patient is someone in his early thirties, married, with three and a half years of previous therapy. He entered therapy smoking two pack of cigarettes a day, taking tranquilizers and sleeping pills, and, in addition to his mental anguish, suffering from stomach distress and headaches. His average time in Primal Therapy was eight months, by which time he felt practically cured. He would never consider entering another therapy and believes that what cures tension and its sequelae is getting to his walled-off feelings. Primal Therapy produces a calm and contentment in him; it eliminates his symptoms and his need for relief habits such as alochol, drugs, and cigarettes. His sex life is less frequent but deeper and more fulfilling. He is a better husband and father simply because he is a better, less demanding human being. He does less than he did before, produces less, is less sociable and enjoys being alone more. He feels more alive and will not struggle with anything or anyone. He is healthy and does not abuse his body. He has no great aspirations, likes to eat and take walks. He is a simple human being.

3. NEUROPSYCHOLOGICAL MEASUREMENTS OF PATIENTS UNDERGOING PRIMAL THERAPY

BY RICHARD CORRIERE AND WERNER KARLE[1]

Introduction to Neurophysiological Research

The following research study indicates that Primal man is truly a new kind of person on this earth. His whole system is less defended, more open and natural. There are many implications of this. For example, body temperature is lower in a consistent way. Rises in temperature reflect women's monthly cycle in a more predictable way because these temperature changes are not contaminated by alterations in tension levels. Thus we have the possibil-

[1] This research was carried out in partial fulfillment for doctoral degrees in psychology at the University of California at Irvine. Partially supported by National Institute of Mental Health research grant MH 12853–04.

ity for true natural birth control. We already have preliminary evidence that Primal women can accurately predict their ovulation period based on temperature readings. It is when women are unnatural, neurotic, that they cannot rely on natural bodily rhythms for internal indications.

Obviously, if temperature is slightly elevated constantly to ward off Primal stress, the physical system is under constant inner attack and will fall prey to disease and death much earlier in life than is normal in evolutionary terms. Primal man should survive longer because he has rediscovered his youth in a very real way. And his brain waves often change after his therapy to resemble a young person's.

It is clear from the research that neurosis is not an "attitude" or set of behaviors. It is a physical, neurophysiologic fact. When a primal patient has his body temperature drop as much as three degrees in a two-hour period (pre- and post-Primal), we are clearly dealing with a revolutionary internal event.

The purpose for undertaking this research can best be explained through the following two points: First, we are psychophysiological beings; that is, our brains and bodies are not separate entities—they are one functioning unit. What occurs in one is reflected in the other. Second, Primal patients reported lower tension levels after therapy. Therefore we would expect to see these changes reflected in the body. In the pilot studies to be reported here, we monitored four simple parameters of change: blood pressure, pulse, rectal temperature, and brain waves. In future, hormone levels will also be evaluated.

The initial results from these pilot studies should be interpreted only as a significant trend which is helping us design new and more detailed research projects. However, we consider this trend exciting enough to report at this time.

DESIGN

Three groups of subjects were run: an experimental group (n = 29), an active control group (n = 10), and an inactive control group (n = 10). The experimental group consisted of Primal patients undergoing their first three weeks of intensive therapy. The active control group was made up of volunteer subjects who followed a physical exercise program for an hour and a half. This program allowed for a self-regulating cycle of rest and exercise. The inactive controls were also made up of volunteers who remained seated for two hours during which they read, talked, or slept.

The reason for having an active group was to rule out the chance that the results of the experimental group were merely due to exercise. On the other hand, the inactive control group was used to eliminate the possibility that lying down and relaxing could produce the same effect as a Primal session.

METHOD

On all groups the following measurements were taken before and after each session: blood pressure, pulse, and rectal temperature. Care was taken to measure each of these parameters at the same time of day for each subject with sophisticated electronic equipment.

RESULTS AND DISCUSSION

Before we discuss the results, let us clarify the meaning of the entries in the figures and tables by explaining the statistics we used to arrive at our significance levels. The Wilcoxon Matched Pairs, Signed Ranks Test, a nonparametric test, was used because it was the simplest and most efficient test for reporting to the general public. The test does not say anything about the magnitude of daily individual changes; it simply tells us whether or not the number of changes per subject during the three-week period was significant, and the direction of significance, i.e., whether there were more negative or positive changes and whether the number of either positive or negative changes was significant. (For example, Table 1 indicates that 13.8 percent of the patients had a significant number of systolic blood pressure increases.)

The first varible we will discuss is blood pressure. (See Table 1.)

We found blood pressure to be an insignificant varible

TABLE 1. BLOOD PRESSURE CHANGES.
This table shows the percentage of subjects in each group who had a significant *number of daily* individual changes during the first three weeks.

A. Systolic Blood Pressure

	Groups		
	Primal Patients	**Active Control**	**Inactive Control**
Significant Number of Decreases	0%	0%	0%
Significant Number of Increases	13.8%	0%	11.2%
No Significant Changes	86.2%	100%	88.8%

B. Diastolic Blood Pressure

	Groups		
	Primal Patients	**Active Control**	**Inactive Control**
Significant Number of Decreases	0%	0%	3.7%
Significant Number of Increases	37.9%	0%	22.2%
No Significant Changes	62.1%	100%	74.1%

in most cases. Consider first the systolic blood pressure. As shown, there are no significant decreases, only a small number of significant increases, and mostly no significant change whatsoever.

The results from the diastolic blood pressure tests are very similar to those of the systolic pressure tests. Diastolic blood pressure differs from the systolic in that it more closely reflects vasoconstriction, i.e., how constricted the blood vessels are. Again, the possible significance of blood pressure changes are not brought out by this test. For people with blood pressure in the normal range, as was the case with most of our patients, blood pressure may be a variable that changes (if at all) very slowly; thus, significant differences will be observed only after, say, six months of therapy.

Evidence for this hypothesis comes from the individual subject analysis of the blood pressure data. In this analysis, we discovered that patients with chronic high blood pressure showed dramatic decreases over the three-week and subsequent three-month periods. In three cases of high blood pressure, we found sustained drops of 38, 28, and 36 points in systolic blood pressure. These drops occured only after the third week of therapy (see lower half of

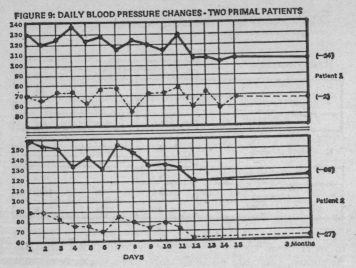

FIGURE 9: DAILY BLOOD PRESSURE CHANGES - TWO PRIMAL PATIENTS

Figure 9 for a sample of one of these patients). As soon as the blood pressure had its first large drop, it then fluctuated between baseline and some lower value until that defense was completely broken. After the defense structure of these three patients was broken, their blood pressure continued to fluctuate—but now in a much lower range, never returning to the initial high levels.

To summarize blood pressure results, it would appear that the most dramatic changes will occur in people with mild essential hypertension. The effect on normal tensive people, if at all, occurs slowly. We found no comparable results in either control group.

Results of pulse measurements are shown in Table 2 and Figure 10. As will become clear in our discussion of pulse changes, this variable is a much earlier indicator of tension release than is blood pressure.

It is obvious that the number of pulse decreases in Primal patients exceeds that of active or inactive controls. But this in itself underestimates the significance of this data. It must be kept in mind that most Primals are very active events. When this is considered in light of the ac-

TABLE 2. PULSE RATE CHANGES
This table shows the same kind of information as Table 2.

	Groups		
	Primal Patients	Active Control	Inactive Control
Significant Number of Decreases	58.6%	0%	44.5%
Significant Number of Increases	0%	30%	.0%
No Significant Changes	41.4%	70%	55.5%

tive control group in which there are no decreases but only increases in pulse rate, we see that a Primal is a unique psychophysiological phenomenon. That is, it is an active event in which pulse rate is decreased! Furthermore, there is no significant number of pulse increases in Primal patients. This is also true for the inactive control, but that is to be expected.

The results from the rectal temperature measurements are interesting. Rectal temperature is a very stable physiological measurement of tension (11). It is not difficult to produce temporary changes in pulse and blood pressure,

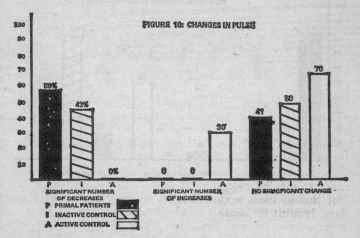

FIGURE 10: CHANGES IN PULSE

SIGNIFICANT NUMBER OF DECREASES
SIGNIFICANT NUMBER OF INCREASES
NO SIGNIFICANT CHANGE
P PRIMAL PATIENTS
I INACTIVE CONTROL
A ACTIVE CONTROL

since these variables respond quickly to external stimulation, but rectal temperature changes usually occur only in correspondence to the circadian rhythm and, to a lesser degree, to physical activity (28). As shown in Table 3

TABLE 3. RECTAL TEMPERATURE CHANGES
This table shows the same kind of information as Table 1.

	Groups		
	Primal Patients	Active Control	Inactive Control
Significant Number of Decreases	82.8%	0%	18.5%
Significant Number of Increases	3.4%	50%	0%
No Significant Changes	13.8%	50%	81.5%

and Figure 11, the active control group responded predictably. Activity produced no significant number of decreases; 50 percent had no significant changes. The inactive control also responded in a very predictable fashion; 18.5 per-

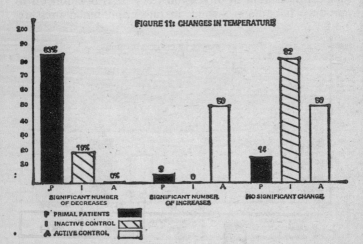

FIGURE 11: CHANGES IN TEMPERATURE

cent of these people had a significant number of temperature drops (this was because of those subjects who slept during their two-hour sessions), there were no significant number of temperature increases, and 81.5 percent had no significant changes.

Surprising enough, 82.8 percent of the Primal patients had a significant number of temperature decreases (again, remember that most Primals are active events and should thus increase temperature as shown by the active control group), only 3.4 percent had a significant number of temperature increases, and 13.8 percent had no significant changes.

The decrease in body temperature from an active event suggests something which can be explained only by bringing together psychology and physiology.

Because the Wilcoxon test did not tell us anything about the magnitude of our temperature changes, we consulted researchers at the University of California, Irvine Medical School, to get an estimate of what in their opinion constitutes a significant temperature change. Present research indicated that a change of .5 degrees or more within a two-hour time span should be considered significant (28). Basing our studies on this information, we calculated the significant (.5 degrees or more) number of temperatures increases and decreases for each subject in each group. These results are given in percentages in Table 4.

TABLE 4. SIGNIFICANT (MAGNITUDE) RECTAL TEMPERATURE CHANGES
This table shows the percentage of subjects in each group who had, in terms of magnitude, significant temperature decreases, increases, and composite increases or decreases (indicated by a plus or minus sign next to the percentage score).

Groups	Directions of Significant Changes		
	Significant Decreases	Significant Increases	Significant Composites
Primal Patients	66.5%	20%	44.8% (—)
Active Control	0%	33.3%	33.3% (+)
Inactive Control	70%	50%	20% (—)

The third column in this table is meant to give an idea of the significance of the *overall* significant temperature changes. Each patient's significant increases and decreases were averaged with respect to sign and to find out whether or not his composite temperature change was positive or negative, and whether or not this composite change was itself significant (.5 degrees or more). The signs next to these percentages indicate the direction of the significant changes.

A composite of zero would indicate that there was no mean temperature change. The composite of the inactive control group of 20 percent temperature decrease is not meaningful. And the active control group actually showed a composite rise of 33 percent; this compares dramatically to the negative 45 percent change seen in Primal patients, because the Primal group most closely resembles the active control. Therefore, in one case there was a rise of 30 percent in the Primal patients a drop of 45 percent. This data supplements and reaffirms the results obtained with the nonparametric significance test. That is, not only is the *number* of negative changes in the Primal group more significant that the control groups, but also the *magnitude*.

As is shown from the data, something unique was occurring in the Primal session. This is visualized in the bar graphs in Figures 9 and 10.

In a three-month follow-up study these results were strengthened by the fact that 80 percent of the patients who were monitored retained the low temperature and pulse rates that were produced during their intensive therapy. Controls in both groups were monitored at the end of three months and found to be the same as they were before the experiment started.

This means what is ordinarily considered normal pulse, blood pressure, and temperature is actually a neurotic norm. The implication is that we will need to rethink man's metabolic norms because medical pathology has been based on neurotic norms.

The last variable—brain waves—remains to be considered. Brain waves were monitored once before therapy, at the end of the intensive three weeks, and three months after therapy had started.

The EEG data we have collected to date also reveals some interesting trends. Five Primal patients have shown considerable reduction in brain activity as reflected in changes in frequency, amplitude, and synchronization, whereas neither of the control groups had any EEG changes.

All recordings were done with four electrodes—two frontals and two occipitals; this yielded a total of 10 channels of information which we used for analysis: (RF, LF, RO, LO, RF-RO, RF-LO, LF-LO, LF-RO, RF-LF, and RO-LO). The observed changes took place in each channel, and thus this data may be generalized for all these regions.

The average frequency range for Primal patients before therapy was 10.3–14.8 cps. After three weeks it was 6.3–11 cps. (a reduction of 4–3.8), and after three months the range was 7.5–11.5 cps. (up from the three-week reading but still a reduction of 2.8–3.3 from baseline). These patients' average frequency baseline was 12.5 cps., and the three-week and three-month figures are 8.9 (a 3.6 drop) and 9.9 (a 2.6 drop) respectively. There was an average amplitude drop of about 15 percent, i.e., the new average amplitude level for these patients was only 85 percent of what it was before. One more important item was observed in the EEG changes. We noticed that those patients whose EEG was generally desynchronized now are beginning to have a very synchronized wave pattern. On the other extreme, one patient had a highly synchronized, fast, and large amplitude wave which is now slower, smaller, and less synchronized. So there are no absolutes.

It is becoming apparent that the new EEG pattern of post-Primal patients is very similar to that of a person in a rested state, i.e., it reflects a relaxed physiological state of being. The most important difference is that patients are very awake and alert when they are producing the Primal restful waves.

We want to emphasize that these readings were all taken in the middle of the day, at the same time of day, and under identical conditions that would best reflect normal waking activity. Thus we attempted to control for any possible fluctuations caused by differences in activation or biological rhythms.

It is possible that the reason the brain is so deactivated after therapy is that as all the defenses go away, less cortical activity is needed to keep the defenses up, thus allowing the individual to feel and be his natural self. The slower, more efficient operation of the brain is reflected not only in the newly found synchrony of the waves but also in the comparatively large drop in frequency, and perhaps more importantly, amplitude.

It is important to state that Primal Therapy produced lasting changes in brain-wave activity, while the changes in the control groups were only temporary.

In our previous research, on meditation, autocontrol of brain waves (called biofeedback), brain-wave driving (alpha drive and theta drive), and hypnotic susceptibility, we found the EEG patterns associated with these states to be fast, high-amplitude, synchronized alpha (8, 12, 18, 19, 20, 30). This is contrary to brain-wave patterns found in Primal patients. Though we had previously concluded from our early research with autocontrol of brain waves, alpha drive, etc., that the brain-wave patterns found were salubrious, we now believe that those patterns were indicative of repression and lack of integration. The previously reported "restful" feelings in such states as meditation and high alpha were the result of *no* feeling. In fact, these states were deceptive because what looked like a restful brain was actually a hypnotized one.

In our previous research in meditative-hypnotic states we could produce a slower frequency wave but the amplitude would increase—as though to compensate for it. By forcing a slower brain wave we believe that we altered the characteristic defense pattern of the brain so that Primal feelings began their ascent. The protective reflex of the brain is to increase its spread and synchrony of discharge.

Brain waves must be considered part of the defense structure. Their synchrony, amplitude, and frequency are an integral part of the homeostasis of the system. To artificially interfere with those natural, cerebral functions is to further throw the system off balance. It would be tantamount to artificially altering the frequency of the heart and pulse rates with drugs. It does not change anything in an integrated neurophysiologic way.

Alpha drive, meditation, and self-hypnosis are similar in that they offer the person a new defense against the Pain. These people do feel better subjectively, but their brains are in fact more activated—giving the lie to that subjective self-deception.

DISCUSSION AND CONCLUSION

While each of the results we have presented is of interest, this data is even more significant when viewed as a whole. The temperature, pulse, and brain-wave decreases indicate that tension is a total physiologic event and, owing. When tension is reduced, those parameters are changed. In essence the organism has slowed itself and cooled down so that it burns its energy at a slower rate (much as when running efficiently, a finely tuned engine consumes less fuel, produces less waste and heat, and lasts longer).

Natural man evolves naturally; he is an open person, not shut down by Pain. An open person has a lower threshold for the recognition of what endangers his life (17). The neurotic has a higher threshold of recognition because of his constant state of stress. With his high level of tension, his body does not differentiate between real and unreal threats. He is continuously reacting neurophysiologically to past Primal threats, rather than responding to present-day reality. He is therefore less adaptive to his current surroundings.

What happens when there is less Primal stress? You have a group of individuals with slower metabolism who make less overall demand on the external and internal environment for life support. For the neurotic to equal that state, he would have to be asleep (9). He would have to be in a defenseless state which only sleep offers.

Because pulse, temperature, and brain waves are part of the defense structure, something such as high temperature—98 degrees or more—cannot be considered as intrinsic to normal man, but has been part of *neurotic* evolution. Patterns of metabolism and brain waves are end points in one's personal evolution and cannot and should not be changed by artifical, transient, external means.

When there is an actual physical assault on the body such as surgery, body temperature rises (14, 16). This permits increased circulation so that nutrients and white blood cells needed to fight disease have more access to the whole system. When stress exceeds certain limits, the temperature defense will rise so high as to kill the organism. In this sense, defenses can kill and are not integral to the human organism, nor are they healthful. This concurs with Labroit, who said: "The defense mechanisms so far from defending our existence, are very frequently the more or less direct cause of death" (14, 16).

When temperature is excessive, the adult may become momentarily psychotic and hallucinate. Lower temperatures, therefore, may be indicative of lessened neurosis. In Primal terms, temperature is commensurate with the amount of physical defense needed. It is one of the major physiological changes to occur under stress, and temperature readings are routinely taken in cases of illness (11).

A defenseless person has a relatively low temperature. This is one indication that his body is not under stress. He is not a self-actualizing neurotic who has found socially acceptable ways to utilize neurotic activation; he is a natural evolving organism.

We can see the practical applications of our hypotheses in the work of Wolf (32). He treated an infant who was having continuous epileptic seizures by reducing his body temperature. As long as the infant's body temperature remained below 98 degrees, there was a minimal amount of electrical activity in the brain. As soon as the body temperature rose to 98, the seizure pattern was exactly the same as before. Here again, we see indications of what an integrated entity the human system is; further, that temperature and brain activity are related in a significant way.

Comments and Speculation by Dr. Janov

We have just completed replicating the Karle-Corriere study at the Primal Institute. The changes shown in the original research in terms of electroencephalography, blood pressure, pulse, body temperature, and heart rate were again confirmed. A control group of university students who were given simulated Primals (who recounted significant feeling events in their lives but did not relive them) showed none of these changes. Controls were measured before and after physical exercise similar to the kinds of physical activity which occur in Primals; there were again none of the changes one finds with actual Primals. It would appear that a Primal, reliving Pain, does, indeed, resolve tension.

We have recently begun an intensive study of a patient referred from a state mental hospital. Preliminary analysis of her daily EEG record, as well as her sleep EEG record, shows that significant changes occur in both these measures daily depending on what happens in Primal Therapy during the day. The daytime EEG changes are not as dramatic as the sleep record. If she had a good therapy day with a completed Primal, most of the measurements decreased. In addition she required much less D-time or REM sleep. If she had a bad day with an uncompleted Primal, she needed more REM sleep. After a good day, she needed as little as 25 percent of the amount of REM time as on a bad day. That is, after a therapy day with unfinished Primals she could require 75 percent more REM sleep. Of course, much research needs to be done with this patient and others in terms of daily measurements. Complete stastical analysis of all the above has not been completed. Until that analysis, we shall have to be content with speculations as to their meaning. One sees very little speculation in the social sciences. Facts are apotheosized while ideas are denigrated. This may be due, in part, to the fact that there has been little "science" in the social sciences, very little that is predictable. The result is a kind of overcompensation in which we have concentrated on the so-called hard data to the neglect of concepts which might tie data together and generate some universal laws about the psyche. The kind of speculation that I think is necessary is not brainstorming; rather it is a willingness to extrapolate from what we see and know into the realm of the possible. It means a willingness to be wrong.

I think that we need to make leaps in the imagination, for it is imagination that can change us from scientific automatons into creative beings. We should take care to differentiate speculation from fact, but we should not be afraid to be what Abraham Maslow calls the "assault troops" of science.

Research with our individual patient indicates that dreams seem to take up the slack of Pain and tension. The more leftover Pain from the day, the more we must dream. This means that the amount of dreaming we need to do is related to the amount of residual tension in our bodies. Conversely, the more tension resolved, the more likely we are to have restful nights. Dreams, therefore, must be seen as neurotic outlets, helping us maintain psychic equilibrium.

We have recently begun a number of research projects, which I shall discuss in a moment. One of the more exciting innovations is the use of a strobe light. By means of a pulsing light, we can alter brain-wave frequencies, a well-established fact. Until now, the main clinical use for the strobe light has been for alpha driving, a procedure in which subjects are conditioned toward a certain wave frequency and we can eventually reproduce that frequency on command by rearranging their thoughts. The alpha frequency is a sign of repression—of an active brain suppressing feelings. Alpha driving can be used to suppress the experience of pain, and it can and has been used to diminish the secretion of stomach acids. Neurotics who first enter Primal Therapy usually have a high stabilized alpha wave. We have discovered that this alpha state continuously decreases as therapy goes on.

We have made another discovery; that there is a "Primal Frequency"—a certain wave frequency brought about by slowing the brain down with the use of strobe lights— which makes people feel. Primal subjects can feel the instant we hit their frequency. They will suddenly start to cry or to writhe, suddenly begin coughing or go into one defense or another. The Primal Frequency is close to but several digits below the stabilized alpha one. For example, if a new patient has a stabilized alpha of twelve, his Primal Frequency will be around ten. If his alpha is about ten, the Primal Frequency may be at eight. This is another way of saying that his feelings lie slightly below his cortical defenses. If we pulse the brain at a faster rate than the Primal Frequency, feelings immediately shut off and the person becomes defended. If we pulse the brain at a slower frequency than the Primal one, we get drowsiness, sleep, or relaxation.

What all this means, first of all, is that there is a "natural" brain rhythm, just as there is sleep and dream rhythm or a menstrual one.

In neurotics, the natural rhythm is altered. Usually, it is speeded up so that our brains are going at too fast a pace. That is why as we become more natural beings, our brain waves slow down considerably. Being oneself, then, means to have a naturally pulsing brain. Feeling humans, it turns out, have much slower brain activity than non-feeling ones because it takes a great many cortical defenses to keep feelings down. Not only that, but the amplitude of the wave is higher in repressed neurotics because it takes so much neural activity to maintain repression of Primal Pains. The brain in neurotics is under great pressure. How this pressure is manifested is more a subject for scrutiny by neurologists. It seems reasonable, however, to assume that it affects everything from thought processes to certain kinds of brain disorders.

One immediate implication of our preliminary strobe work is that it is a quick and efficient way to tranquilize people. That is, we can reproduce the effects of electro-analgesia (see Part I) by flooding the brain with so many impulses that it must shut down *all* feeling in order to defend itself. Far more important, however, are its implications of becoming a kind of Primal Machine for refractory cases. When someone is really shut down and is having a difficult time in Primal Therapy, it is possible to bring his brain waves down into the feeling level and into Primals. When this has been done with non-Primal patients, what happens is that the person becomes "spaced out." He does not feel—or seems up tight, funny, uncomfortable, delusional, etc. The amplitude of his wave rises at the point of feeling to aid in the defense and to produce, thereby, the spaced-out experience instead of the Primal one. Slowing down the waves of Primal patients usually results in the feeling. It does not always result in a connected feeling, however. We have patients press a buzzer when we reach their Primal Frequency. When that happens, a patient may say, "My body is feeling, but my head cannot figure out what it is." Or he may say, "My throat is suddenly so tight; I feel like I'm going to choke. It feels like there's a cry trying to come up." If we encourage the patient to talk at that point (just a few words), the content of the feeling will become apparent, and the result is a Primal. Or, if we hyperventilate the patient then, he will begin to wail and cry.

Whether the Primal is verbal or nonverbal, very early or later on in life, will depend on the Primal Frequency. If the Primal Frequency is down around two, close to an infant's stabilized frequency, then the Primal is apt to be nonverbal and very early. If the patient is fairly new, and his Primal Frequency is around eight, chances are his Primal will be about something later on in life. As the patient progresses, both his alpha and his Primal Frequency drop.

We may have to rethink our norms about brain waves just as we have to take a new look at the norms of body temperature. It may be that we have established our norms on neurotics; so that the norms of real people are quite different from what we think. We know that infants' waves are very slow, and that as we get older and the brain develops and becomes myelinated the waves speed up until we get alpha and beta. But one major factor in why this happens may have to do with the increasing amount of cortical defense children must develop in order to cope with their environment which will not allow them to feel. If this were not so, then how else may we explain why the stabilized brain waves of advanced Primal patients are so similar to those of children?

Perhaps a word is required about childrens' brain waves.
Perhaps a word is required about children's brain waves. pleasure and pain). These waves predominate until a child is five or six, when they share equally with alpha

waves. After the age of six, alpha waves predominate. This may mean that feelings are preeminent until we become five or six years old and then defenses begin their ascent. In other words, the major split which I believe occurs at that age shows itself in a literal split in the brain wave pattern between alpha and theta—between feeling and repression. Once a child enters his teens, repression becomes stabilized along with his alpha waves. Primal patients often return to the theta range after therapy.

Because infants and young children do not have high alpha, do not have an abundance of active cortical mass to aid in repression, they can be easily overloaded. Take just the speed of the mother's speech, for example. If she is pulsing the young child's brain at a speed that is not natural for him (if she is talking too fast), then he must deny his own brain rhythm and try both to comprehend and speak at his mother's level. He must have the "fast answers" she demands. If the mother can feel, she will sense the brain rhythm of her child and speak in that rhythm with a loudness which can also be integrated smoothly. Too fast and too loud speech, in itself, can produce Primal overload. A therapist who does not feel may talk "out of synch" with his patient, and a feeling patient is immediately put off by it. The speech may not match the patient's cadence or it might be too soft or too loud.

This all may seem strange to many people. But if we consider how open an infant is, and how crucial it is for him to accommodate himself to his parents for survival, then we see that synchronizing himself to his parents is an automatic survival mechanism. Though the memory of the specific accommodation is often lost in neurotics, what we see later is inordinate anger when someone talks too much or too fast, or gives too many orders at once. The person, in short, is reacting to that very early denial of self, though he has no conscious recognition of it.

I should hasten to add that the notion of a Primal Machine in a therapy as natural as Primal seems incongruous. But too many of us have been made into machines already, so that anything we can do to help those kinds of people along will be investigated. For the vast majority of patients, no machine is needed. All they need is a place to feel.

In terms of brain processes, the post-Primal patient is very like the young child. As frequency and amplitude of brain waves decrease, the possibility of overload becomes greater. We see this empirically in those patients who report that the smallest noise bothers them. They cannot stand restaurants with a great deal of tumult; whereas before they may have spent many of their nights in noisy piano-bars. They are more receptive to the slightest stimulus both day and night, and thus are awakened more easily by noise. Having an undefended brain means to be sensitive in the true sense of the word. We often say that we cannot "penetrate' insensitive people; and in terms of the neurotic brain this is a literal fact. A very active neurotic brain shuts out a great deal. That is why one often has to hammer home a point with neurotics in order to make them understand. That is also why they can stand tremendous noise (say, of loud music).

In sleep research we find that though the D-state or REM stage is not the deepest stage of sleep, it is the most difficult time to arouse a person. I would assume that because the brain is so busy defending against feelings during this period it takes a greater stimulus to penetrate and awaken.

A defended brain requires more drugs to quiet it; whereas in post-Primal patients the smallest stimulus— a cup of coffe—is immediately perceived mentally. It is probably no accident that we stabilize high alpha waves in our teens, which is also the time when many serious physical and mental ailments begin, ranging from epilepsy to schizophrenia.

The need for research in Primal Therapy is great. We need to follow Primal patients for years to see how well our findings hold up. We need before and after biochemical studies to see exactly what changes are taking place inside us on a chemical level. We need help from outside scientists who can help find new parameters for study. Thus far, the results are exciting and tend to validate Primal Theory. But there is a great deal to know, and that knowledge can come only from a multidisciplined approach. Those involved in Primal Therapy know it works; now we are faced with the task of proving it.

BIBLIOGRAPHY

1. Altman, P. L., and Dittmer, D. S. (eds.). *Biology Data Book*. Washington, D.C.: Federation of American Societies for Experimental Biology (No. 6555), 1964.
2. Barker, Wayne. *Brain Storms*. New York: Grove Press, 1969.
3. Benzinger, T. H. "Heat Regulation: Homeostasis of Central Temperature in Man," *Physiological Reviews*, 49:4 (1969), 671–687.
4. Brazier, M. A. B. *The Electrical Activity of the Nervous System*. New York: Macmillan, 1958.
5. Brown, C. C. (ed.). *Methods in Psychophysiology*. Baltimore: Williams and Wilkins Co., 1967.
6. Cameron, D. E. "Heat Production and Heat Control in the Schizophrenic Reaction," *Archives of Neurology and Psychiatry*, 32 (1934), 704–711.
7. Crozier, W. J. "The Distribution of Temperature Characteristics for Biological Processes; Critical Increments for Heart Rates," *The Journal of General Physiology*, 9 (1925/26), 531–545.
8. Engstrom, D., London, P., and Hart, J. T. "Hypnotic Susceptibility Increased by EEG Alpha Training," *Nature*, 227 (1970), 1261–1262.
9. Guyton, A. C. *Textbook of Medical Physiology*. Philadelphia: W. B. Saunders Co., 1966.
10. Harned, H. S., Herrington, R. T., and Ferreiro, J. I. "The Effects of Immersion and Temperature on Respiration in Newborn Lambs," *Pediatrics*, 45:4 (1970), 598–605.
11. Harrison, T. R. (ed.). *Principles of Internal Medicine*. New York: McGraw-Hill Book Co., 1962.
12. Hart, J. T. "Autocontrol of EEG Alpha," *Psychophysiology* (Abstract), 4 (1967), 506.
13. Himwich, H. E. *Brain Metabolism and Cerebral Disorders*. Baltimore: Williams and Wilkins Co., 1951, 146–168.
14. Huguenard, P. "Technique and Results of Artificial Hibernation: Its Place in Present Day Practice," *Report*

to *National Congress of French Anaesthetics*, October 4, 1952.

15. Jacobson, E. *Biology of Emotions.* Springfield, Ill.: Charles C Thomas, 1967.

16. Laborit, H. *Reaction Organique a l'agression et Choc.* Paris: Masson & Cie., 1952.

17. Lacey, J. I., and Lacey, B. C. "Some Autonomic-Central Nervous System Interrelationships" (Unknown Source).

18. London, P. Galbraith, G., Cooper, L., and Hart, J. T., "EEG and Hypnotic Susceptibility," *J. Comp. & Phys. Psych.*, 72 (1970), 125–131.

19. London, P. Hart, J. T., and Leibovitz, M. "EEG Alpha Rhythms and Hypnotic Susceptibility," *Nature*, 219 (1968), 71–72.

20. London, P., Leibovitz, M., McDevitt, R. A., and Hart, J. T. "The Psychophysiology of Hypnotic Susceptibility," in *International Symposium on Psychophysiological Mechanisms of Hypnosis*, ed. by Leonard Chertoh. New York: Springer, 1969.

21. Maulsby, R. L., and Edelberg, R. "The Interrelationship Between the Galvanic Skin Response, Basal Resistance, and Temperature," *J. Comp. and Phys. Psych.*, 53:5 (1960), 475–479.

22. McClure, J. H. "Newborn Temperatures: II. Temperature of Premature Infants," *Obstetrics and Gynecology*, 9:6 (1957), 642–645.

23. McClure, J. H., and Balagot, R. C. "Newborn Respiration," *Obstetrics and Gynecology*, 17:2 (1961), 243–247.

24. McClure, J. H., and Caton, W. L. "Newborn Temperature: I. Temperature of Term Normal Infants," *J. Pediat.*, 47 (1955), 583–587.

25. Milnarich, R. F. *A Manual for EEG Technicians.* Boston: Little, Brown, & Co., 1958.

26. Ruch, T. C., and Fulton, J. F. (eds.). *Medical Physiology and Biophysics.* Philadelphia: W. B. Saunders Co., 1960, 992–1004.

27. Siegel, Sidney, *Nonparametric Statistics for the Behavioral Sciences.* New York: McGraw-Hill, 1956.

28. U.S. Dept. of Health, Education, and Welfare. *Biological Rhythms in Psychiatry and Medicine.* Public Health Service Publication No. 2088.

29. Venables, P. H., and Martin, I. (eds.). *Manual of Psychophysiological Methods.* New York: John Wiley and Sons, 1967.

30. Wallace, R. K. "Physiological Effects of Transcendental Meditation," *Science*, 167 (1970), 1751–1754.
31. Walter, W. G. *The Living Brain*. New York: W. W. Norton & Co., 1963.
32. Wolf, P. H. "Motor Development and Holotelencephaly." (Unknown Source).
33. Wyke, B. *Principles of General Neurology*. Amsterdam: Elsevier Publishing Co. Lt., 1969, 503–505.

Sample Post-Primal Interviews

INTERVIEW 1

INT: How old are you now?

PT: Fifty-one.

INT: Marital status?

PT: Divorced.

INT: How long have you been divorced?

PT: Eighteen or nineteen years.

INT: What happened to your first wife—do you ever see her?

PT: She has remarried. I saw her a couple of years ago. She was in Los Angeles on a visit and called me.

INT: And there were no children out of that marriage?

PT: No.

INT: You have never had a child?

PT: No.

INT: How long were you in therapy?

PT: Ah, about five months—a little more than five months.

INT: And how often did you come after the first three weeks?

PT: Three times a week.

INT: If you had a word to choose to describe where you are, what word would you choose—cured, partially cured, helped, the same or worse?

PT: Ah.

INT: Or your own word.

PT: Well, immeasurably helped. I really don't know what cured means. And I don't see the therapy as something that kind of cures you so that you never have another problem. I see it as a means of coping with problems, so it has solved many, many of my problems. But daily living brings on fresh problems, and I find that I am now able to cope with them.

INT: Did you have previous therapy—what type?

221

PT: I had over eight years of psychoanalysis and over two years of psychotherapy.

INT: At the time you were in those therapies, did you feel helped?

PT: In the sense that having someone to talk to was a help. It kind of kept me alive, just the continuity of it, knowing that there was a meeting coming up and as long as you have a meeting coming up I guess you have some degree of hope. But at the same time, I—while I was in psychoanalysis I became an alcoholic.

INT: Did you leave voluntarily—which one was first, the analysis or the therapy?

PT: I had one year of a psychiatrist when I was around twenty-one, then I had the eight years of psychoanalysis when I was well in my forties—and, well, I became—I was committed to a hospital as an alcoholic, and when I was released from the hospital my analyst told me he could do nothing more for me. And he recommended, however, that I have treatment, and my analyst and M.D. jointly recommended my psychiatrist.

INT: Before you came to therapy here, to Primal Therapy, did you have any specific ailments?

PT: Physical ailments?

INT: I seem to recall that you had high blood pressure. Is that something that you had before?

PT: Well, this is really complicated. Let me go into this in some detail.

INT: O.K.

PTS Ah, I first went into analysis because—well, let me go back even further. When my wife divorced me, I began to suspect shortly after that I had a heart problem or difficulty of some kind. My heart was skipping beats—beating rapidly, etc.—and I was quite willing to die. It didn't concern me at all, but I didn't. And years went by, and I began to have some success as a writer, and I thought, well, maybe I had better stick around. So, I went to an M.D. and I said I think I have heart trouble, and what can I do to help it. And he could find nothing wrong with my heart, so he suggested that I had emotional problems and from that I went into analysis. Well, at that time my heart rate went 125–130 times—beats per minute.

INT: At what age?

PT: Forty-odd. I would lie in bed at night expecting it to stop at any instant. Ah, it would skip beats and I would just wait, wondering if it was going to start again. It was quite frightening. Then, after a couple of years of psychoanalysis, the skipped beats went away and the rapidity of the pulse declined somewhat. When I would have my blood pressure taken, it would sometimes be quite high; other times it would not be. When I came into Primal Therapy, my pulse rate was in the high eighties to nineties. In the three-week period at the beginning it went down to in the seventies, and all through Primal Therapy it continued to go down.

INT: What was the lowest it ever went down to?

PT: Well, the lowest I have ever taken it was 56.

INT: Is it now in the fifties and sixties?

PT: I think the last time I took my pulse it was around 60.

INT: Did your doctor notice anything remarkable about that?

PT: Yeah, he thinks it is quite fantastic.

INT: What about your heart?

PT: I have no problems, nor did I ever have as far as that—

INT: I see. It was just an anxiety attack probably. And then your pulse rate. For how long was it in the high eighties— how many years of your life, or don't you know?

PT: I would say that for ten years it was seldom below a hundred, and then for the last five or six years of my analysis it went down to in the eighties.

INT: Well, now that you have been through all of this, had all of that, would you consider entering other therapy?

PT. No.

INT: What specifically in Primal Therapy helped you?

PT: Getting in touch with my own feelings, which I had successfully walled off for so many years.

INT: Didn't anything like what happened here ever happen to you in any of your therapy sessions?

PT: No, never, never.

INT: That's really hard to believe. I mean, it just seems like you would have some kind of—

PT: Well, if you mean crying, yeah, but the kind of crying that I did in analysis was kind of a gentle sadness and it didn't go to any root causes.

INT: And the crying you did here?

PT: It went right to the core of the whole thing.

INT: Would you care to comment on the first three weeks of your therapy and the therapist?

PT: Well, the first three weeks I found very, very rough. Ah, I contemplated walking out on the therapy in the first three weeks.

INT: What made you stay?

PT: In part the money, the commitment, and in part, I didn't know anyplace else to go. If I didn't do it here, it seemed to me there was no other therapy that could do it. And I was pretty well persuaded intellectually and in a way, emotionally, that this therapy would do it.

INT: What criticisms do you have of Primal Therapy?

PT: Well, I didn't come prepared.

INT: Haven't you ever thought about it?

PT: Yeah, I found some of the noise very hard to take. And I felt it distracted me from my own work. And I finally got earplugs so I wouldn't be so disturbed by other people. Yet I must admit earlier in the five-month period, ah, it did not bother me so much.

INT: How would you improve it—the therapy?

PT: I don't know.

INT: You're a big help. How has your behavior changed, if it has?

PT: For eighteen or nineteen years I have been divorced. Since getting out of Primal Therapy, I have been going with a woman and we are planning to get married in the fall. And I see her every day, I guess. And it would have been intolerable to me prior to therapy.

INT: What would have been intolerable?

PT: Seeing anyone every day.

INT: Why?

PT: Oh, that means I'm stuck, I'm—I'm—

INT: Trapped?

PT: Yeah. I'm—before coming into Primal Therapy I was on sleeping pills and tranquilizers and antidepressants, and now I'm not. I haven't had a headache since coming into Primal Therapy. And I used to have them constantly—that means daily.

INT: And you haven't had any?

PT: Not one.

INT: That's fantastic. You are completely off all things?

PT: Ah, I occasionally take aspirin because of the pain in my shoulder due to playing badminton. That's some kind of arthritic. Even Primal Therapy can't do anything for it.

INT: No.

PT: Let me add one other thing that is kind of curious, and I don't think it's going to shake the world to its foundation, but as a result of Primal Therapy, I am a better chess player.

INT: Oh?

PT: The reason for it is now when I play chess I am able to concentrate better on the game and able to devote my intellect to the game rather than my emotions, to the frustrations of wanting to beat somebody.

INT: Did you smoke before you came to therapy?

PT: Well, no, not immediately before, but yes, I have been a very heavy smoker.

INT: Do you smoke now at all?

PT: No.

INT: It wasn't Primal Therapy that stopped you from smoking?

PT: No.

INT: Do you drink now?

PT: No.

INT: But you did before?

PT: Well, I'd stopped before coming into Primal Therapy.

INT: How long before coming into Primal Therapy had you stopped smoking and drinking?

PT: I'd stopped drinking—I stopped approximately two years before, and then I had a relapse and ended up in the hospital again—as an alcoholic again.

INT: You would just go all day, every day?

PT: I was drinking a quart a day.

INT: Do you think that if you were at a party and you were having, say, a martini, cocktails, or whatever, that would change—would shift you into going back—relapsing?

PT: I don't think so, but I would not accept a drink—or take a drink.

INT: Why not?

PT: Ah, I have no desire for it. I don't like the—drinking and feeling that drinking induces has a very unhappy connotation for me—an unhappy association for me—and I'm much happier knowing where I am and what's going on.

INT: What about drugs? You already mentioned you're not

taking any of the other ones. Do you do anything else—any other drugs, such as smoke grass?

PT: No, I never have.

INT: And apparently you don't overeat.

PT: No.

INT: Do you feel the need for any of the things we talked about?

PT: Sometimes I want sweets. Sometimes I would like to have a whole cake or ice cream.

INT: What about smoking? Do you ever wish you had a cigarette?

PT: No.

INT: Has your sex life changed since you have been in therapy?

PT: Well, yes, It's quite active and simply that I'm getting—there is more of it.

INT: Mainly because you now have somebody you really like.

PT: Yeah.

INT: I didn't mean to put those words into your mouth. Was there anyone before that you were able to have a good time with sexually?

PT: Well, while I was drinking I spent years just picking up girls in bars, and it was a pretty unsatisfactory kind of sex life.

INT: What comment could you make on tension before and now—has that much changed or a lot changed?

PT: Ah, it has changed—the quality of the tension has changed. There is tension now, but for different reasons. In the past it was tension that grew out of a general sense of insecurity and unhappiness and doubt about myself and the world in general. Now I have tensions too, but they come out of the—in fact I am still having trouble with my work and I am very concerned about it. It is a very realistic concern and there's a lot hanging on it. I'm not going to marry a woman I can't support. Ah, I have a consciousness now of what I consider good writing to be, and it's very hard to attain it. I'm a very harsh critic of my own work. Ah, and it's very frustrating not to be content with what I do.

INT: So you would say maybe that the therapy has in a way made you understand more deeply what good quality is but made it harder to achieve, or makes it hard to achieve, because you haven't—

PT: Well, let me put it in other terms—I think we may be saying the same thing. I used to write situation comedies and without much difficulty and was very successful at it. I am no longer content to write the kind of situation comedies I used to write. I want to write something more meaningful and it's no longer easy.

INT: I see. Do you still Primal?

PT: Yes.

INT: How often?

PT: Well, I don't know how to answer that. What is a Primal? My notion before coming into therapy was one thing and going out is quite another. I cry more openly and I cry very, very often—I would say once a day on an average. Do I have a—what I consider an effort to hook up with something in my own past, no. As a conscious effort to have a Primal session. When I first stopped coming to meetings, I would do that two or three times a week. Now perhaps I do it once in ten days.

INT: Is there anything else you want to say about anything? Let's see—the last part is a description of your everyday life, which I guess you are telling me—has it changed a great deal?

PT: Well, my level of tension, I think it is important to say this, has reduced tremendously. I am able to be quiet much more than I used to be. Before coming into Primal Therapy I had to get out of my house—just to get out. Now it is no longer necessary. I leave when I have something to do. I am more content to lead a life that is homespun.

INT: And you're content with it?

PT: And also I find myself not—I keep drawing away from people I once thought were permanently important people in my life.

INT: Anything else you want to say, before we end this?

PT: No, I think I would just ramble.

INT: I really appreciate your coming.

INTERVIEW 2

INT: How long were you in therapy? How often did you come to group after three weeks?

PT: I was in Primal Therapy for a continuous nine months, then I attended groups once in a while. After the first three weeks, I attended group at least once a week and occasionally had an individual session.

INT: Have you been cured, partially cured, helped, the same or worse? Explain.

PT: Prior to Primal Therapy I would have described myself as a highstrung, nervous, overly emotional, frustrated woman. I never *knew* if I was right or wrong about anything. I never *knew* what I was feeling. I had a terrible temper about almost everything my oldest daughter did and often spanked her violently. I didn't like her, didn't want her, and had no patience with her. I felt guilty that I couldn't treat either of my children the way I thought they should be treated—that I couldn't care about them—and I thought something was wrong with me because of that. I was afraid that I was going to eventually kill both of them to keep myself from feeling what was really wrong with me. I was sick. My disconnected childhood feelings were always rising to be felt, but I didn't know what I was feeling, nor did I want to feel them. Whenever I was upset, hurt, mad, or confused, I tried to connect the feelings to things that had happened today, but I was never really sure why I felt so miserable.

Of all that, I am cured. I am now a calm person. I know what I feel is right. When I am upset, it is always because something happens today which reminds me of another time—years ago—when my parents hurt me and I kept myself from feeling the hurt. At those moments I make the connection—I feel the hurt and remember what caused it just as though it was happening at that moment. There is never any doubt about what I am feeling. Once the connection is made, the "upset" is over. I never "lose my temper" anymore because there is no temper to lose—the unfelt, unexpressed anger I felt toward my mama and daddy was finally connected to them, and there is no longer any need to direct those feelings toward my children in a feeble attempt to rid myself of the resulting tension. After all those years I finally felt all the pain my parents caused me, the pain that was so unbearable that I couldn't stand to feel it as it happened, the pain that always made itself known to me by making me think something was wrong with me, the pain that messed up my life because it wasn't connected to what caused it. It was my parents who caused me to hurt, and it was because I wanted and needed so much for them to want and love me that I settled for just the belief that they did. It was my parents who had made me miserable, not my children. It was a better mama I wanted, not a better child.

I originally sought therapy because I felt my husband didn't love me and was going to leave me. This was another example of a disconnected feeling from my past. The feeling component was there, but I was constantly trying to make the wrong connection. It was my daddy who didn't love me and wanted to get rid of me. Once the feeling was connected to him, there was no doubt that it was right. That was not the case when I tried to connect the feeling to my husband. I always doubted it because it didn't feel right. Since those Primals, I have never thought about my husband loving or not loving me.

My life now is smooth, without tension and struggle. Before Primals my life was full of chaos and seemingly insoluble problems.

INT: What previous therapy have you had?

PT: I was in regular therapy for two and a half years with an existential psychologist. It was a complete waste of time and money. I thought at the time that it had helped me, but all it did was help me control my feelings and involvement in "upsetting" situations. After Primal Therapy, my feelings no longer made me miserable—they are *me*. "Upsetting" situations are welcomed because they are the triggers for connecting my life—my feelings.

INT: Any specific ailments relieved or cured?

PT: Specific ailments cured were *tension*, hemorrhoids, pimples, pulled muscles in lower back due to tension, chronic anxiety, acute attacks of fear (fear of dying or being "no good"), a tendency toward hypochondria (my doctor bills are much less).

INT: Would you ever enter another kind of therapy?

PT: Never, nor would I recommend any other therapy to anyone. Other therapies do patchwork—patching leaks of the unsuccessfully repressed feelings. Thinking and reasoning are the defenses taught by other therapies. Real sense can be made only when the feelings are felt. People seek therapy for a *cure*, and I feel that Primal Therapy is the only one that can offer just that—a cure for the disconnection of feelings.

INT: What specifically about Primal Therapy helped you?

PT: Connecting my feelings to the original source of the feeling—the original cause—was what specifically helped me. Reliving those moments—feeling as though I was back there—a child—was the only way the connection could be made. Without the insistence and encouragement of the therapist to feel and connect, I would not have been helped.

INT: What criticisms do you have of Primal Therapy? How would you improve it?

PT: My first three weeks of individual sessions were very painful, yet pleasant. It was a pleasure to finally make those long-sought, yet resisted, connections—to finally feel and know the source—the cause of my misery. During those three weeks the major changes took place within me. For the first time I felt what it was like not to be tense. My body seemed to fall into place as though my bodily functions—hunger, digestions, defecation, urination—had been freed from a jail-keeper. For the first time in my life I felt hungry (I had been underweight). My constipation ceased. My body began to grow and my hands and feet weren't cold all the time. Still, the feelings inside me hurt terribly. Often I didn't want to feel them, but I didn't seem to have a choice. The therapist seemed brutal and insensitive at times because he wasn't protecting me from my feelings but instead encouraging me to feel them. He encouraged me to "sink into the feeling," and though I would be scared and doubtful, I would later be amazed that the feeling connected to a memory which had long ago been forgotten.

My therapy was in the birth years of Primal Therapy, and groups were very bad. Only one person at a time was on the floor, and those waiting their turn for the floor either lost that chance to feel or didn't feel their feelings in the fullest intensity. I'm glad groups aren't like that anymore.

I can't think of any criticisms except that it is very expensive, although not so by comparison to other therapies. It is very painful, but if it weren't it would do no good, since it is all that unfelt, disconnected pain that made us need the therapy.

INT: Would you recommend it to others?

PT: I would definitely recommend Primal Therapy and have done so. It is discouraging, though, since the waiting list is so long that those to whom you recommend it can't get in.

INT: How have your behavior and life style changed?

PT: Except for the anger I've already explained, the tension, my behavior hasn't changed very much. The biggest change as a result of my Primals is how I feel inside. My Primals caused an inner revolution within me, and the result is not easily discernible. My reasons for doing whatever I do have changed. I always did what I thought I should do—what I thought I might be loved for or not loved for. Now I do what I want to do and don't do what I don't want to do. I say what I feel, not what I think I should say.

My life used to be full of hassles, messes, upsets, problems, hurt feelings, anger, and a million things I didn't like. Now, there isn't anything in my life that I could call a problem. In short, I never struggle. I was miserable before and am never miserable anymore. I never enjoyed myself before but really enjoy myself now, at whatever I am doing. I seldom get upset, hurt, or angry, and when I do, it is always the beginning of a Primal. I still Primal and probably will for a long time if not for the rest of my life. Sometimes I Primal at least once a week for a few weeks, then other times I might go for a month or so without Primaling. It depends on whether or not I am triggered.

INT: Do you now smoke, drink, take drugs, or overeat?

PT: No.

INT: Do you feel the need for them?

PT: No.

INT: Describe your sex life.

PT: Before Primals I didn't always have an orgasm, and the kind I did have were nothing like what I have now. Orgasms before were tense, high-strung, but I described them as pleasant. Now they are totally encompassing. The orgasm is felt throughout my whole body—not only in my cunt or in my clitoris. As I look back at my sex life before Primals, it was in general not very pleasant. Fucking my husband meant that he wanted me and I was saved for the time being of having that "unwanted" feeling triggered. Sex, now, is pure feeling. It is just sex—not symbolic reassurance of being loved or safety from old, unfelt, hurtful feelings.

Yes, I feel tension sometimes. I sometimes have tension just before a Primal. I am also tense when I do something I really don't want to do but force myself to do it because it has to be done. I was tense when I was in college for a year because I really didn't like it there. I would have

dropped out sooner but I needed a master's degree to do
what I thought I was going to be doing later. I simply
didn't like it and was tense because I did it in spite of my
feelings.

When I was in regular therapy I wrote a description of
my everyday life. I wish I could compare it with mine now.
The difference between this one and the old one would be
unbelievable.

Bibliography

Beecher, H. K. "Increased Stress and Effectiveness of Placebos and 'Active' Drugs," *Science*, 132:91 (1960).
———. "Measurement of Pain," *Pharmacological Review*, 9:59 (1957).
———. *Pain in Men Wounded in Battle*. Bull. U.S. Army Med. Dept., 5:445 (1946).
———. "Powerful Placebo," *Journal of the American Medical Association*, 159:1602 (1955).
Bergamini, Ludovico, and Bergamasco, Bruno. *Cortical Evoked Potentials in Man*. Springfield, Ill.: Charles C Thomas, 1967.
Cannon, W. B. *Bodily Changes in Pain, Hunger, Fear and Rage*. 2d ed. New York: Appleton, 1929.
Handy, Rollo. *Methodology of the Behavioral Sciences*. Springfield, Ill.: Charles C Thomas, 1964.
Hanna, C., Mazuzan, J. E., Jr., and Abajian, J., Jr. "An Evaluation of Dihydromorphinone in Treating Post-Operative Pain," *Anesth. Analg.*, 41:745–760 (1962).
Hardy, J. D., Wolff, H. G., and Goodell, H. *Pain Sensations and Reactions*. Baltimore: Williams and Wilkins, 1952.
Kolodny, A. L. "Importance of Mood Amelioration in Relief of Pain: A Controlled Comparative Study of Three Analgesic Agents," *Psychosomatics*, 4:230–233 (1963).
Kolodny, A. Lewis, and McLoughlin, Patrick T. *Comprehensive Approach to Therapy of Pain*. Springfield, Ill.: Charles C Thomas, 1966.
Kuntz, Albert. *Visceral Innervation and Its Relation to Personality*. Springfield, Ill.: Charles C Thomas, 1951.
Lasagna, H. "The Clinical Measurement of Pain," *Annals of the New York Academy of Science*, 86:28 (1960).
Lowry, Thomas P. *Hyperventilation and Hysteria*. Springfield, Ill.: Charles C Thomas, 1967.
Madow, Leo, and Snow, Laurence H. *The Psychodynamic Implications of the Physiological Studies on Dreams*. Springfield, Ill.: Charles C Thomas, 1970.
Schramp, J. R., and Schramp, H. M. "Variability of Pain Threshold in Man," *Journal of Dental Research*, 25:101 (1946).
Smith, W. Lynn, and Philippus, Marion John, *Neuropsycho-*

logical Testing in Organic Brain Dysfunction. Springfield, Ill.: Charles C Thomas, 1969.

Vandam, L. D. "Clinical Pharmacology of the Narcotic Analgesics," *Clin. Pharmacol. Ther.*, 3:827–838 (1962).

Wittenborn, J. R. *The Clinical Psychopharmacology of Anxiety.* Springfield, Ill.: Charles C Thomas, 1966.